MEDIEVAL COSTUME

&

HOW TO MAKE IT

DOROTHY HARTLEY

MEDIEVAL COSTUME
&
HOW TO MAKE IT

A REVIEW OF THEIR SOCIAL ASPECTS ARRANGED
UNDER VARIOUS CLASSES AND WORKERS
WITH INSTRUCTIONS FOR MAKING
NUMEROUS TYPES OF DRESS

WITH INTRODUCTION & NOTES BY
Francis M. Kelly

200 Illustrations

GREENPOINT BOOKS

Angelico Press © 2016
This edition by Greenpoint Books,
an imprint of Angelico Press,
is an unabridged reprint of the first edition
published by Charles Scribner's Sons, 1931

For information, address:
4709 Briar Knoll Dr.
Kettering, OH 45429
angelicopress.com

978-1-62138-997-2 (pbk)
978-1-62138-996-5 (cloth)
978-1-62138-995-8 (ebook)

Cover design: Michael Schrauzer

INTRODUCTION

PYGMALION ENJOYS LACING UP GALATEA
[Bodl. Liby. MS. Romaunt de la Rose, 15c.]

UNLESS I am much deceived, interest in the apparel and general outward appearance of our ancestors is gradually growing at once more widespread and more intelligent than in any previous era. I would specially underline this word 'intelligent'; since, particularly from the 'Romantic' movement of the early nineteenth century, there has long existed a vast deal of half-baked *Schwarmerei* in connection with the 'good old times' in all their supposed accidental outward manifestations. It went hand in hand with indifference to, if not aversion from, the unvarnished truth of historic record, as much from intellectual indolence as from ignorant conceit. It found expression chiefly in 'fancy-dress' balls and parties and in so-called 'historic' pageants, such as made fearful the years before the War. Considered merely as a social pastime it is harmless enough in all conscience : it affords a number of leisured folk an excuse for gratifying an innocent vanity and for imposing upon their neighbours' reluctance to say ' No.'

We cannot, I regret to say, as yet declare : *nous avons changé tout cela* ; it is neither likely nor specially important that ' Society ' should ever be denied the right of entertaining itself in the spirit it finds most amusing. Fancy-dress need after all be no more than its name implies ; glaringly inaccurate ' historic ' pageants have on the other hand no excuse for their being. All too late it is beginning to be realized, slowly indeed but no less surely, that the historic evolution of dress and personal ornament offers a wide field for methodical study ; that it is in fact a science and can be made to subserve worthier ends than those of mere amusement. In its degree the dress of the past is no less the outward reflection of its age than, say, architecture, and its educational value should be hardly less.   Indeed it is perhaps scarcely too much to say that we shall but imperfectly apprehend the true inwardness of many events and personalities as long as we are unable to visualize them in their proper habit and surroundings.   From the purely educational point of view, historic truth is no less desirable in this department than in any other.   In this respect the stage and, above all, the cinema have unlimited possibilities if rightly directed.   Actually the travesties often served up to the public are too glaring to be even funny.

The value of a good grounding in the history of costume does not stop here.   It is one of the most valuable means we possess in assessing the value of artistic attributions.   In old *genre* painting, and especially in portraiture, innumerable are the instances where it might well prove the determinant argument for or against a suggested identification. In a recent book-review I read : '. . . many a false datal attribution in the world of collecting might have been obviated by a precise knowledge of bygone dress ' ; and elsewhere—' For them [*sc.* art-critics] a nice knowledge of humdrum details, of sleeves or curls or cravats, would be a godsend, as an aid to and corrective of intuition.'   This was a cardinal precept—scarcely remembered, much less followed—of the late Sir George Scharf.   But of recent years, mainly on the Continent, yeoman service has been done by (among others) Messrs. Adrien Harmand, Paul Post, F. van Thienen and Mmes. E. de Jonghe, Hélène Dihle and Ottilie Rady.   Even heraldic indications are a far less reliable index than costume, since they may well, even where they are old, have been added *après coup*—a relatively easy matter.   It would require no very profound study of costume to save the intending collector in many cases from wasting money on rank impostures.

While we are not so unreasonable as to expect the average person to have leisure or a taste for antiquarian researches, he on his part has a right to look for clear-cut and accurate guidance from those who presume to ' put him wise ' in this as in any other department of knowledge.   Vague generalities such as fill the usual run of ' costume-books ' are apt to be of very little use as soon as definite detailed information is sought on any particular point.   It is a wholesome experience for the would-be expert to be compelled to answer off-hand the questions of the ordinary man in the street.   It will do him good to realize how unprepared he often is to deal with problems which suggest themselves quite naturally to his unsophisticated neighbour.   He will never learn anything worth knowing till his own abysmal ignorance is brought home to him.   For the ordinary reader it is a difficult matter to pick and choose from the heterogeneous mass of matter offered for his consideration. We have therefore a right to demand that the guide-books to which he is referred should supply no 'information' that is not accurate, methodical and clear-cut.

It is a thoroughly unsound, though very common, practice in books on English costume to partition off particular modes by reigns, as if in so many watertight compartments. One particular type of dress is treated as characteristic of the whole of a particular reign and no other. Thus Charles I, whether at his marriage to Henrietta Maria (1625) or on trial at the bar of the House of Commons (1649), must borrow his wardrobe from van Dyck. It so happened that that artist's residence at Court (1632-41) corresponded almost exactly with one of the most elegant *ensembles* of masculine attire that ever fashion evolved, but one equally alien to the starched and corseted figures of Buckingham's day and the ungainly deformations that came into vogue during the Civil Wars.

As Miss Hartley has aptly insisted, before attempting to reconstruct in our mind's eye the outward appearance of our forebears it is necessary to familiarize oneself pretty accurately with the general surroundings in which they moved and had their being. Account must be taken of their position in the social scheme, of age, place, season and the particular circumstances that govern their activities. In our present age of progress a certain drab uniformity seems more and more to be the mark of at least the male sex. Except on formal occasions there is nothing whereby we may tell a duke from an *endimanché* dustman. Far otherwise was it in our ancestors' time. A doctor, a lawyer, a merchant, a husbandman had each his appropriate habit, differing in its degree from that of the man of rank and fashion. We should not allow 'romantic' conceptions of the Middle Ages to warp our common sense. I shall not readily forget witnessing a stage-performance in which a plain 'Cavalier' squire set out a-hunting upon his estate resplendent in gold brocade, salmon-pink ribbons and billowing lace. Is it necessary to suggest that an Elizabethan noble, say, would, as a matter of course, cut a very different figure when in attendance at Court from the same man taking his ease on his estate or travelling to and from town ? Perhaps it may be worth while to point out that, down to a comparatively recent date, gentlefolk past the meridian of life tended to adhere in their declining years to the modes of their prime. In our age of easy and rapid communications we hardly realize how slowly fashionable innovations percolated through to the provinces and countryside. Thus it would be nothing out of the way for an old lady in 1568 to wear an old-fashioned ' gable ' hood of the type that went out of vogue about 1541. Nor should it be forgotten that, apart from sumptuary edicts (which, as a matter of fact, were largely disregarded), the various classes were broadly distinguishable by their attire. Nowadays there is no outward mark distinguishing doctor from patient. In ordinary life soldiers, sailors, lawyers and professors all affect a drab uniformity of mufti ; baroness and barmaid dress alike so far as taste and means allow.

' What do they know of England who only England know ? ' The quotation holds good in costume as elsewhere. A proper understanding of dress and fashions in England postulates some general acquaintance with corresponding and contrasting modes on the Continent at large. Even within our island frontiers their systematic study recaptures for us a whole vanished cosmos. In the following pages Miss Hartley, whose excellent series (written in collaboration with Miss Margaret M. Elliot) *Life and Work of the People of England* (6 vols., A.D. 1000-1800) has earned golden opinions, gives us a further taste of her quality. She shows clothes and their accessories not as inanimate exhibits fit only for a museum, but as a vital part of the life of yesterday, man's companions in labour and leisure, pleasure and pain. Dress after all was never invented to be a studio-property, nor yet to find occupation for antiquaries. Learning and industry will not carry you very far if you do not in a measure apprehend the anatomy and character of costume. The ideal expert would be a blend of antiquary, artist and—practical tailor. To reconstruct satisfactorily the dresses of the past, the methods of the past must be rediscovered and materials (and measurements) akin to the originals employed. The stock methods of the modern costumier will not answer[1] ; on the other hand traditional forms and methods still preserved in remote country parts are often suggestive. The ' working patterns ' given in certain costume-books rarely work out convincingly, indeed some are quite unpractical.

Miss Hartley's book is expressly *not* a history of costume ; she has attained effectiveness and freshness by adopting a subject classification on social lines. It is rather a serious endeavour to resuscitate, so far as may be, a certain number of representative types of mediæval society with their characteristic apparel as something lived in, worked in, played in. Society at large rather than ' Society ' with a capital S

[1] Cf. HARMAND, Adrien : *Jeanne d'Arc. Ses costumes, son armure* (p. 118) ; Paris, Leroux, 1929. This work, by the way, more nearly approaches the suggested ideal than any other I know.

furnishes the patterns, though many of the forms are basic and can readily be adapted to modes current in fashionable circles. Some of these, notably the long hose and the full skirt of the Middle Ages, are models of ingenious contrivance.

Still, without attempting anything like a history of costume, a few words may not be out of place concerning the main lines of its evolution. The dress of clerics and professional men on the one hand; on the other of the agricultural and labouring classes, develop by imperceptible degrees over long periods. The former is prescribed by established tradition, the latter dictated by considerations of convenience. It is among the smart set and the well-to-do that we must seek the changes of form that hall-mark successive epochs. The graphic material at our disposal previous to the Conquest is on the whole inadequate both in quantity and quality, nor is it easy within even a half-century to assign alterations in fashion. From the Crusades dates a notable change. Evidence external or internal or both enables us to follow successive modes with increasing accuracy step by step. Though radical changes in the general outline are rarely abrupt, it is perhaps reasonably correct broadly to divide costume from the Crusades [1] to Bosworth, as under.

(Note in passing how the male influences on fashion are often more marked and varied than female.)

I.—About 1100 to 1340, which might almost be described as an age of SHIRTS and SHAWLS. Stateliness as expressed by trailing draperies and ample folds was the ideal of the ruling classes for all full-dress occasions. In the first half of the twelfth century this was exaggerated almost to grotesque lengths, but by the last quarter of the century these excesses had gradually been pruned away, and costume from its close till well-nigh the middle of the fourteenth century remained on the whole simple, dignified and comely. The early Crusades introduced a number of Byzantine elements, but these were of brief duration.

II.—About 1340-1385. With this period begins the reign of the tailor. Dignity was largely superseded by jauntiness. The general aim of the modes is to show off and emphasize the lines of the body and even to ' build up ' the figure. Costume in the main however is elegant and free from exaggeration.

---

[1] Till quite recently our ' star ' witness for the dress, arms, etc. of the Conquest has been the Bayeux Tapestry; but as nowadays competent critics are widely at variance with regard to its actual date of execution and we have no satisfactory testimony of the latter part of the eleventh century to substitute in its place, we make the Crusaders our starting-point.

III.—About 1385-1460. This era introduces most of the freak-forms popularly associated with the ' Middle Ages ' at large. Skimpiness and superfluity of material jostle one another often in the same suit of apparel and the edges of the draperies are freely slittered into tongues, scales, leaves, etc. Fantastic fashions in hair and headgear appear in great variety for both sexes. France and then Burgundy is the centre of fashion.

IV.—About 1460-1485. Length and height are the dominant features, and Burgundy continues to call the tune. Costume is no less eccentric than before. The masculine figure suggests a skinned frog ; the ladies are (literally) ' of a high stomach,' their heads crowned with towering structures of varying outline. In the last few years of the period, broad square forms begin to invade the figure. But with the accession of the Tudors a new era starts in the life of the people of England. The conquest by the Moslems of Constantinople in 1452 is commonly accepted as the *terminus ad quem* of what we know as the Middle Ages. But in France the rivalry between the Crown and Burgundy, in England the death-struggle between Lancaster and York, retarded the effects in the West of humanism and its attendant culture and kept alive a last flicker of the old feudal spirit which died on Bosworth Field in 1485.

F. M. K.

NOTE.—Is it necessary to point out that such freaks of fashion as masses of trailing drapery, towering head-dress and ' piked shoon ' tapering into rat-tail points could be indulged in only by those of a leisurely habit and in a position to be waited on by tirewomen and lackeys ? The working classes ignored them perforce.

THE OLD CLOTHES DEALER
Note gowns hung over pole
[B.M. Roy. MS. 10. E. IV. 14c.]

THE publishers gratefully express their thanks to the following for permission to reproduce the subjects illustrated : C. W. Dyson Perrins, Esq., D.C.L., F.S.A., pp. 25 (B), 30 (C and D), and 56 (A), from the Gorleston Psalter ; Rev. F. Sumner, 46 (B) ; F. H. Crossley, Esq., pp. 46 (D) and 51 ; Brian C. Clayton, Esq., p. 105 (B) ; to the authorities of the British Museum and the Victoria and Albert Museum ; and to the Librarians of Bodleian Library, Oxford ; Trinity College, Cambridge ; and Trinity College, Dublin, for facilities for including a number of subjects from their great collections.

A proportion of the Plates of Manuscripts are taken with occasional variations from subjects illustrated in ' Life and Work of the People of England,' by Dorothy Hartley and Margaret M. Elliot.

CONTENTS

NOTES ON MATERIALS AND THEIR TREATMENT

MATERIALS.—Most costume-books give lists of materials in use during definite periods and all costumes should be studied with an understanding of the material of which they were made. During certain dates the *widths* of materials were fixed by law, and this has a definite effect upon the costumes of that period (or perhaps the costumes caused the laws). The short skimpy little robes that whisk through the Saxon MSS. lose all their character if carried out in stuff of wider loom width, and for the skimpy type of short robe, material 18-24 inches, *i.e.* that made by a single-handed worker on a small loom, is used.

Actually the richer materials, the velvets and silks, seem to have been very like those in use to-day, but the chiffon and soft gauze fabrics should be mistrusted : the mediæval gauze was probably of a crisper, more net-like texture, and though ironing was probably used, a more convincing quality can be obtained by wetting and stretching out the fabric till dry.

This treatment can be used for elaborately folded veils and head-dresses, and when they are unfolded and worn they have just that angular stiffness seen in the miniatures. The gold gauze and coloured veils that become so popular towards the end of the fourteenth century seem to have been of softer folds.

Linen may be used, as the makes are similar, and the wetting and folding process can be carried out successfully.

In some of the MSS. you may find frills, so regular that they appear to be accordion-pleated, and these may have been close folded over straws, as some French nuns still treat their coifs to-day.

There are also long crinkled garments worn by the women that have a crêpe effect. To copy these, make up the dress, gathering as much fullness as possible into neck and shoulder seams, and mark the height of the waist. Soak the gown in water (a little gum added is an advantage if the material is cotton ; linen does not require it) and wring it out lengthways, twisting it into a tight long rope. Bind it very tightly around with cords at the waist line and leave till dry.

When shaken out and worn the robe shows delicate creasing, with closer tight cross-creasings where the waist came under the extra binding cords.

Woollen material of all sorts may be used, provided the weave and colourings are suitable. The patterns would be direct lines and squares, as a tartan ; some of the wool was extremely coarse and long-haired, so that the rougher makes approximate to loose tweed rather than close flannel.

Remember the enormous amount of give and shrink in any woollen fabric and study whether some of the close fits (especially in hose and jerkins) may not be the result of stretching and weaving rather than subtlety of cut.[1] Leather may be used freely and dyed, gilded, worked and sewn into many costumes.

Beware of trying to get the same effect with modern leather substitutes or cloth. The texture and substance are absolutely different. If very thin skins or imitation leather *must* be used, paste them down on felt before cutting, but it is better to use it less and have the real thing. Skins and furs are a great asset, and may be worked and clipped as desired ; a favourite device was black and white lambskin cut into checkers or diamonds. The best way to do this work is to baste the two skins together and cut both together to *half* the pattern, the alternate pieces completing the other half exactly.

Cords, girdles, ties, etc. were made of mixed materials. Long narrow girdles appear to have been sometimes hand-woven back and forth, while the threads were held stretched between two pillars. The plain, twisted wool-girdle of the earlier pictures takes more material than one supposes ; an easy way to make this girdle is to take a strand of the material (coloured wools) twice the length and about twice the thickness required, twist from each end in opposite directions until tight, and then slack the tension at the ends. Allow the ' twist ' to run up the entire length and complete the girdle.

---

[1] In certain country districts of the Continent the peasants still make and use hand-stuffs locally woven on primitive handlooms and sufficiently elastic to be made up into hose on mediæval lines. (Information received—*experto crede*—from M. Maurice Leloir, President of the Société de l'Histoire du Costume, Paris.)

KNIGHTS TILTING
Note construction of Barrier and Stands   [B.M. Roy. MS. 14. E. IV. 15c.]

THE LADIES HAND THE KNIGHT HELMET AND SHIELD
[B.M. MS. Luttrell Psalter, 14c.]

ROYALTY

OUR English royalties are best found ' in character ' on their effigies in Westminster Abbey, at Fontevrault, and the cathedral churches of Worcester (King John), Gloucester (Edward II) and elsewhere in more or less contemporary sculptures. It should be remembered that coronation robes and the official habits of their office soon became traditional and were little affected by current modes. Judicious research among illuminated MSS. will yield a deal of valuable information.

Every detail should be corrected and decided upon, before an inch of the costume is made. For State ceremonies and historic occasions the costumes are often described by eye-witnesses with minute exactness which must be followed. Therefore in this section we give the traditional robes most generally useful. For resting figure (page 5, No. 5) the first garment would be a silk or linen vest and breeches (= drawers), over this a linen slip reaching below the knees ; over this, for warmth, a woollen under-robe may be worn. The first *visible* robe is of plain linen or silk, ankle length, with long, fitted sleeves. This may have bands of embroidery. Over this a shorter tunic with wide shorter sleeves (page 5, No. 4) which may be of the greatest richness and ornamented with bands of embroidery and gold work. A long heavy girdle (not to be confused with the sword belt) holds all to the figure, and the natural movement of the arm pouches the robe slightly over the waist. Hose and shoes of simple make and a plain gold circlet complete the figure. In the photo (page 3 (B)) and the MS. (page 4 (B)) from which the robe is taken the elderly king wears a light linen coif, materially increasing his comfort without detracting from his dignity. This is specially helpful where a romantic and fantastic crown is designed. The square cloak (page 5, No. 1) is the height of the figure, approximately 6′ × 6′. Adjust the two clasps and strap *on* the figure. It is simple in outline and forms excellent straight graceful folds. The circular cloak (page 5, No. 3) spreads better around a rotund or active monarch ; it also may be clasped on the shoulder, and another version, knee-length, may be effectively swung around your youthful king, when he goes hunting in the Forest of Arden. The oval cloak is a good historical example for brocades, and the diagram shows how the cuttings from the circular end arè replaced to form the fronts and continue the pattern correctly. Another cloak frequently to be copied, especially of the fourteenth century, looks extraordinarily difficult, but is actually the most simple of all, being a perfect circle with a head-hole in the centre. Sometimes you will find a hood attached to the neck-opening, slits for hands, or larger for arms and sometimes the whole cloak slit down the front. The wearers frequently poke their heads through neck or arm-opening indiscriminately and gather the material into pleats over shoulder or elbow. Therefore when studying and copying these voluminous robes, try always to translate them in terms of the plain square or perfect circle rather than conclude at once they are some complicated pattern.

Kingly shoes are usually cut on the same lines as those worn by their subjects.

Note.—Never weight cloaks ; use heavy material. If necessary, use an interlining, but in this case sew it all over into one material and avoid it where possible. Fold circular capes by rolling around the circle and hang up by the neck end of the roll; with square cloaks, roll two sides inwards towards the back unless it is desired to show the lining, when it is as well to store the cloak rolled outwards to train the folds to open that way.

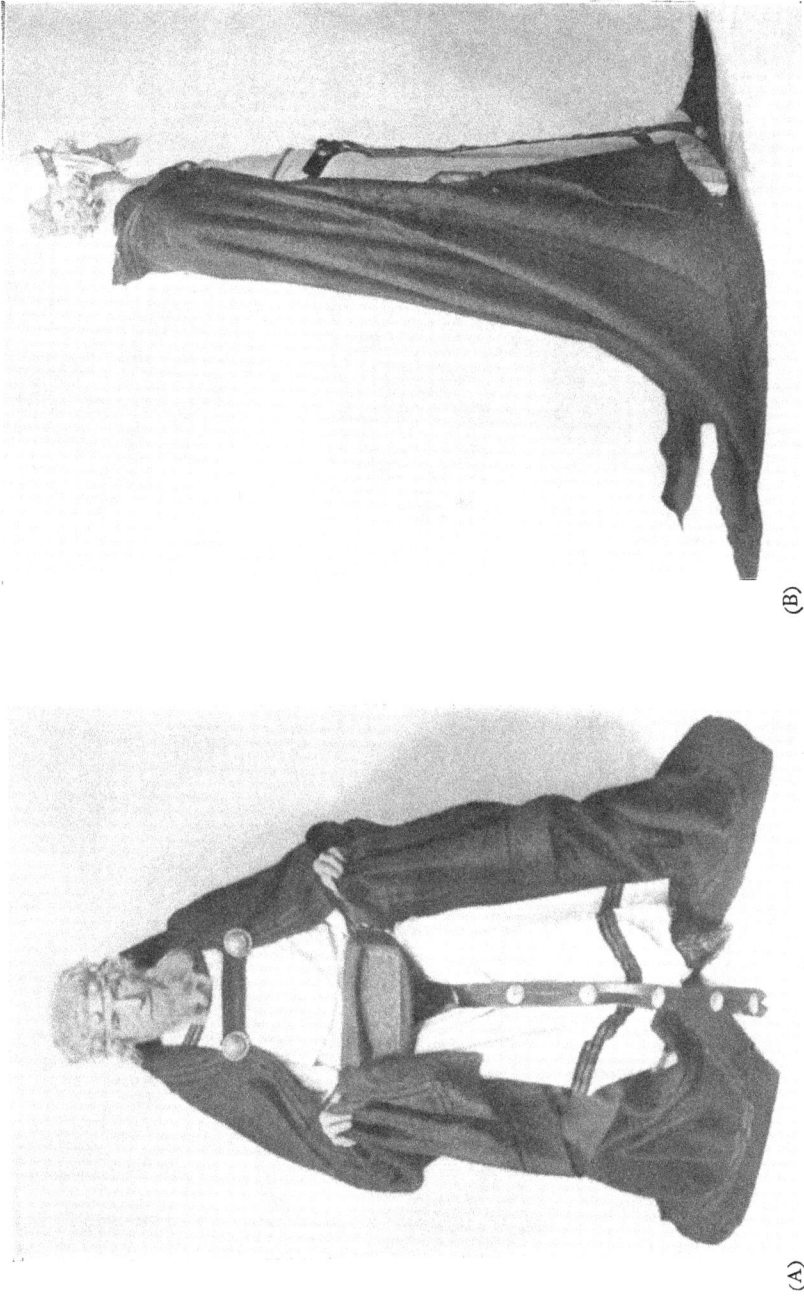

(B)

(A)

A KING. COSTUME BASED UPON THE 14C. ROBES IN FIG. (B), PAGE 4

For the White Robe see page 5 (No. 4)

For the Square Cloak see page 5 (No. 1)

(A)   (B)   (C)

(D)

(A) ROBES OF DIGNIFIED SIMPLICITY; IN CONTRAST TO ELABORATE CROWNS OF GOLD
[B.M. Roy. MS. 20. C. VII. 14c.]

(B) THE HEAD-DRESS AND COSTUME THAT SUGGESTED ROBES ON PAGE 3
[B.M. MS. 14c.]

(C) THE KNEELING PRESENTATION BEFORE A GREAT LORD
(Also note the Jester and Window Seat)   [B.M. Facs. 197, 15c.]

(D) STUDIES IN COSTUME AND POSITION, FOR NOBILITY AND CHURCH
(Also note the Pointed Shoe on the right)   [B.M. Roy. MS. 14. E. IV. 15c.]

ROYAL COSTUME

Square Cloak worn by a king

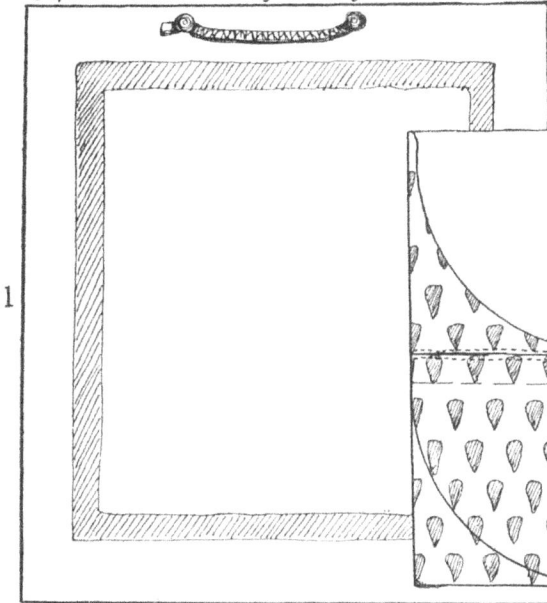

Other arrangements of SQUARE CLOAK.

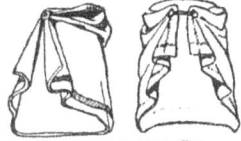

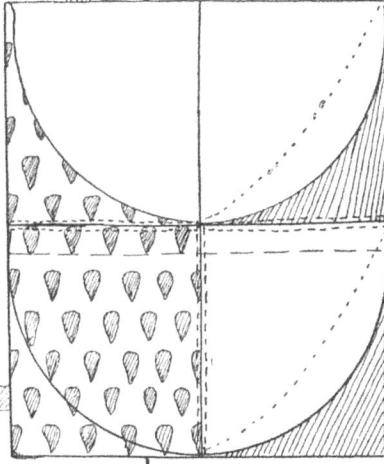

1

2

Oblong Cloak cut out in patterned material

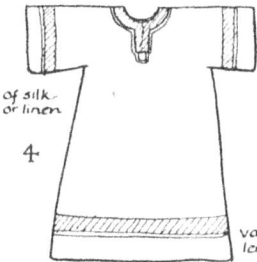

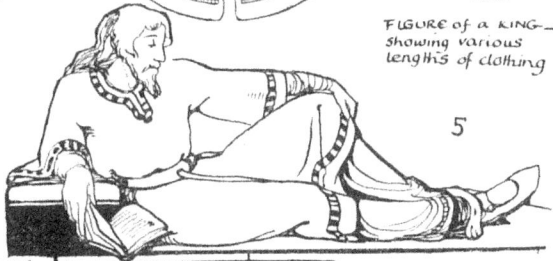

Circular Cloak

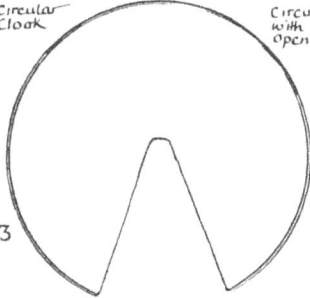

Circular Cloak with neck opening

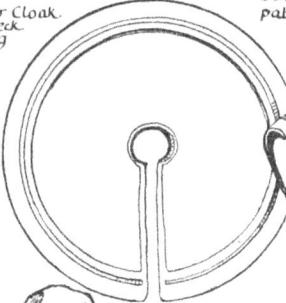

3

4

of silk or linen

various lengths

FIGURE of a KING showing various lengths of clothing

5

RELIGIOUS ORDERS

THE religious orders must be carefully distinguished from the ordinary secular clergy : the parish priests under the direct jurisdiction of their diocesan or bishop. Not till about the tenth century were they definitely constituted into orders ; but their origins go back to the early centuries of established Christianity, and they derive on the one hand from the hermits, on the other from the true monks or coenobites. Although they took vows (of chastity, poverty, etc.) they were not *essentially* priests, especially at the outset, but rather bodies of men primarily devoted to working out their salvation (and that of their neighbours) by prayer and contemplation allied to good works.

The orders of the Middle Ages are divided into (1) Monks ; (2) Canons Regular ; (3) Military Orders ; and (4) Friars (='Mendicant Orders'). The archetype and earliest of orders is that of St. Benedict, which definitely took shape at Monte Cassino in A.D. 529. St. Augustine brought the Benedictines to Saxon England in 597. Their offshoots, the Cluniacs and Cistercians, reached England respectively before 1077 and in 1127 ; the Carthusians were settled in Somerset by 1222. The Friars are a creation of the thirteenth century. Friars differ from Monks principally in that, beyond their actual houses, they have in principle no property, even corporate, but live entirely (in theory at least) on alms. Also their work was individual and lay mainly outside of their houses, whereas the monk or canon laboured corporately within. Also their respective organizations and interdependence differed. The chief orders of Friars were the Dominicans (or Black Friars) established here by 1221, the Franciscans (or Grey Friars) 1224, and the Carmelites (White Friars) before 1245. The Friars played in the nature of things a far more ' popular' rôle in mediæval life than the Monks, being brought into continual direct contact with the populace at large, to whom they appealed for the means to exist, and to whom they ministered indiscriminately. The Franciscans' object was to succour the poor, the sick, the ignorant and the outcast; the Dominicans went about preaching the Gospel to whoever would stop to listen. For that reason the Mendicant Orders figure more prominently in popular art and literature from the thirteenth century down than the Monastic Orders. To go into the minutiæ that distinguish the habits of various subdivisions of each order one from another and the modifications that took place at particular dates would carry us beyond the scope of the present work. Some few data may be given by which certain orders can be readily recognized. The Franciscans wear all brown (originally of a greyish tone, later snuff-coloured) and are girt with a knotted cord (hence the French name, ' Cordeliers '); the Dominicans a black cloak and hood over a white gown and scapular; the Carmelites, originally striped grey and brown, presently adopted a white cloak and cowl over brown. The Benedictines are all black, the Cistercians and Carthusians all white, etc. To most of these correspond female orders, whose habit is largely adapted, at least in colour and material, from their respective masculine prototypes.

The distinguishing marks of the military orders—Hospitallers and Templars—and of the Canons Regular require separate study. In so far as any of the ' Regulars '—*i.e.* of the ' Orders ' as opposed to the secular or diocesan clergy—were full-fledged priests, they shared with the seculars the vestments appropriate to the priestly rites : alb, amice, stole, maniple, chasuble, dalmatic, cope, etc. These again should be studied as liturgical vestments pure and simple, since they are only worn ' on duty.' Originally they derived from more or less popular garments in general lay use. Only in the early Middle Ages do they become stereotyped for purely liturgical wear, each with its particular function : their *symbolism* is of much later date. Thus the *chasuble*, the distinctive mass-vestment of the priest, almost certainly derives from the late Roman *paenula*, a poncho-like cloak, chiefly used in travelling and rough weather. The *maniple*, at first a mere folded handkerchief, presently became more ornamental and then a mere token of ritual functions. The clergy are rarely represented on effigies or brasses except vested for the Eucharist : this is only to be expected, for both the deceased and his friends would account his sacrificial ministry his highest claim to honour. It is worth noticing how beautiful are the liturgical vestments of priest and prelate from the late twelfth to the mid-fourteenth century in form, proportion and decoration, when compared with later forms, which have neither grace nor convenience to recommend them. One is glad to note within the present generation a wholesome tendency to reaction in the matter of church vestments. Notably the episcopal mitre and the priestly chasuble are recognized to be meaningless travesties of their noble thirteenth-century prototypes, and there seems a hope that we may see them soon generally restored to a more seemly pattern. It may be added that the final and worst deformations are essentially post-mediæval.

F. M. K.

(A)

(B)

(C)

(D)

(A) St. Thomas Aquinas Preaching   [B.M. Facs. 60, late 15c.]

(B, C, D)   Groups of Religious in Various Ceremonies: Preaching, Teaching,
Investiture, etc.

(B) [B.M. Cott. MS. Nero C. IV. 12c.]   (C) [B.M. Roy. MS. 16. G. VI. 14c.]

(D) [B.M. MS. 15c.]

(A) [Bible Moralisée. B.M. Facs. 169, late 13c.]

(B) [Bodl. Library MS. Douce 118, 14c.]

(C) [B.M. MS. Addl. 39843, about A.D. 1300]

(A) BLESSING THE CHURCHYARD [V. and A. Mus. Facs. Heures de Milan, 14c.]

(B) FIGURES OF CHURCH DIGNITARIES [Tomb of Philippe le Hardi, Dijon, early 15c.]

CLERKS

THE LEARNED.—These disputant clerks on p. 15 (A and B) are copied from a MS. The gown is simple and plain from neck to hem with plain inset sleeves fitted at the wrist, around which frequently pokes down the white shirt, which may also work up at the neck in stressful moments. The cloak is simplicity itself, but very effective. Page 17 shows the making. Two lengths of cloth, each slightly gathered in the centre around the neck, meet in a plain join on each shoulder. *The shoulder seam should not be gathered but plain,* and should be long enough to reach well over the shoulder joint. This is the whole secret of the hang of this cloak, for it gives the elbow-lift shown on the left figure and causes the loose folds to move and sway with every movement of the shoulder or heave of the chest and to flap wildly and expressively around the outflung arms. The high collar is a straight length of material sewn on and folded over, and forms a circle, wide enough to slip easily over the head. As seen (page 17, No. 1) the width of the material which makes the two sides of the cloak is generally about right for the collar. This gown is usually rusty black. The dishevelled locks of heated argument are shown in the photos (page 15,) but if desired an impressive cap may be made after pattern, page 17, Nos. 3 and 7. To make this, make a tube of thick felt (or a hood), the diameter of the head, and the length from top of head to nape of neck. Slip this over the face and head with its single seam running perpendicularly down the front. The head is then fitted by means of a single seam running up the forehead over the top of the head to the back of the skull, and a horizontal slit cut across the back below the base of the skull. This slit should be taken up till the cap fits the bulge of the head very closely. The face opening may next be marked out with chalk close above the eyebrows and down in front of each ear. A single cut up the face-seam then releases the victim and the face-hole may be carefully cut to frame the learned features with good effect. If this explanation deters your victim from having his face in a bag while you pin up the back of his head, reassure him. In practice the fitting does not take a minute and it is the easiest way to get a truly good fit for the individual head. The close neat fit around the features is very effective.

PROPERTIES FOR THE SCRIBE.—By the end of the fourteenth century are found spectacles with thick horn rims, eyeglasses with jointed hinge ; a book, of which the binding is elongated at the top to form a bag with a knot at the end, slips under the belt, and strong clasps and studs hold all secure ; a purse made of two semi-circular strips and one long one of leather, simple and small as becomes a philosopher ; DESK FITTINGS : a good steep slope with a firm soft surface (felt or leather), sheets of parchment, weighted cords to hold parchment in position. These weights will be seen hanging down at the back of the desk, front or back ; large ink-bottle, small ink-bottle, water-bottle and powder-bags for ink, reflecting globe (for artificial lighting), duster, penwiper, rules, a cloth to throw over the desk, and spare sheets of parchment. *N.B.*—Scribing is a double-handed action, the ivory rule in the left hand pressing down the resilient parchment close to the soft pen nib point,—the quills usually short, large flowing feathers impractical. When copying, the book or parchment is above or to the side as convenient. When a clerk is reading to the scribe he sits below him and rather behind.

ILLUSTRATIONS (page 16).—The hole in the side of the desk was a useful store-box for dusters, etc. The figure in a fur cloak wearing gloves is not a scribe, but suggests a useful costume. The knob on the end of the schoolmaster's cane is a decorative picture of its bang ; the rod would be an ordinary straight one.

(A) (B)

(C)

(A) & (B) TWO ASPECTS OF THE STUDENT'S CLOAK SHOWN ON PAGE 17.

(C) DISPUTANT CLERKS WEARING THESE ROBES AND CLOAKS, MADE BY THE PATTERN
ON PAGE 17 [B.M. MS. Burney 275, 14c.]

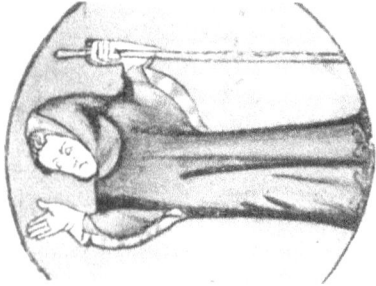

(C)

(B)

(E)

(D)

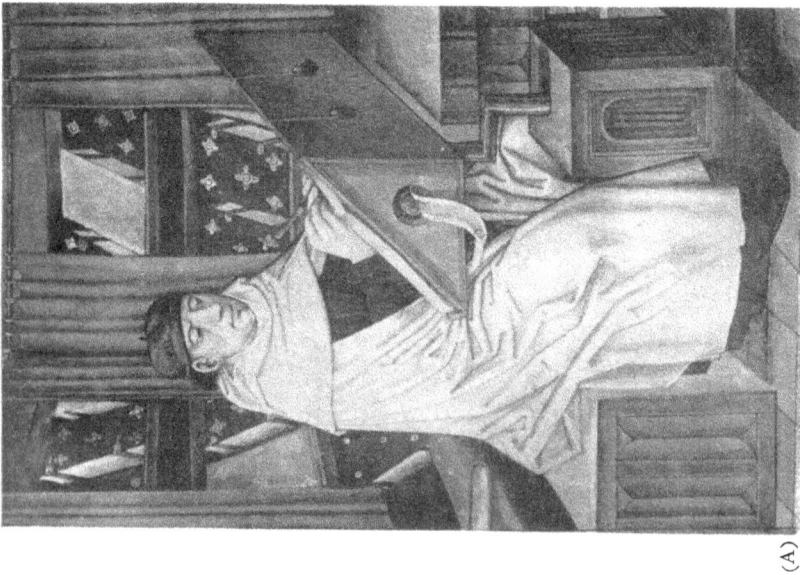

(A)

(A) SCRIBE AT DESK. Full description in text [B.M. Roy. MS. 14. E. 1, 15c.] (B) A STUDY OF COMPLETE REST [Bodl. Liby. Douce MS. 15c.]

(C) *Not* A CLERK, BUT THE FUR CLOAK SUGGESTS A USEFUL ROBE FOR AN ELDERLY MAN [B.M. MS. Arundel 83, 14c.]

(D) THE STUDENT'S ROBE SHOWN ON PAGE 17 [B.M. MS. Burney 275, 14c.

(The knob at the end of the stick is a pictorial representation of the 'bang' [B.M. MS. Addl. 18852, 15c.]

(E) ANOTHER WRITER OF LESS MONASTIC TYPE [B.M. MS. Addl. 18852, 15c.]

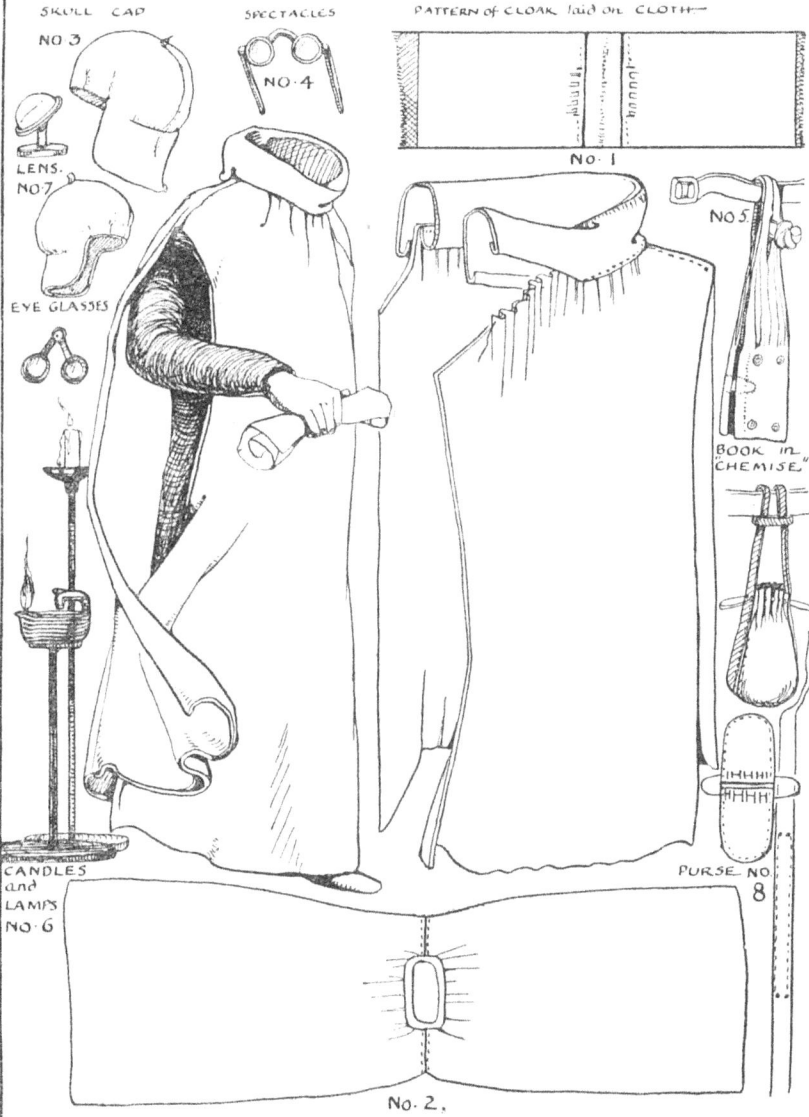

PATTERN OF THE CLERK'S GOWN

SKULL CAP
NO 3

SPECTACLES
NO·4

PATTERN of CLOAK laid on CLOTH

No· 1

LENS.
NO·7

No 5

EYE GLASSES

BOOK in
"CHEMISE"

CANDLES
and
LAMPS
NO·6

PURSE NO.
8

No·2.

PATTERN of the CLOAK, made up and shown flat.

MEDICAL AND SCIENTIFIC FOLK

THE photo (page 19) shows a plain dark gown made of two lengths of cloth; the simple sleeves are set in perfectly plain along the side seams as shown (page 21, No. 1). At the bottom (page 21, No. 2) the material is laid on the cloth and (page 21, No. 3) is the pattern of the sleeves. When these are joined from the wrist upward it will be seen a small triangular piece is left over at the armhole; set it in quite plain before the side seam of the robe is joined up, you will find it moves on the arm loosely and comfortably. See that the wrist fits neatly. The neck is hollowed slightly and may show the linen under-slip (this may also slip down a little at the wrist, looking almost like a cuff). The whole robe is held into the figure by a broad strong belt, to which the doctor's purse and book may be attached. The white coif is a plain straight piece of linen tied under the chin with two strings, and shaped to fit the head down a back seam. In making: tack up the coif, tie the strings under the chin, and *then* fit the back seam A, B, A, page 21, while actually on the head. In no other way can you get the individual close fit. A slight comfortable fullness over the ears is obtained by turning the corners back over the looped chin strings in tiny triangles (about one inch). The almost unnoticeable gathering thus formed makes the coif much more comfortable than when the string is merely sewn on exactly at the point. It is worth while taking some trouble over the coif, which was worn by nearly everybody throughout the thirteenth century. It was always of white linen. The apron is a single straight strip of white linen with a neck slit cut across, and side fastenings. Do not shape this neck-hole in any way. A variant is shown on page 20, where the neck is hollowed into a circle; the difference will be seen at once. The basket (page 21) holds the inevitable glass urine bottle. Above are two medical instruments. A gown, cap, apron, an accommodating leather wallet, and a warm cloak (page 16 (A)) would dress the doctor for most occasions.

ILLUSTRATIONS AND PROPERTIES.—Page 20. (A) Late thirteenth

THE MEDICAL GOWN ; MADE BY THE PATTERNS ON PAGE 21

The original gown was in two shades of grey homespun woollen cloth with dull black leather belt.   The covering was of narrow width thick white linen cloth.   The model's hair was black ; his complexion sunburnt, and the bottle, purposely chosen, of greenish glass.

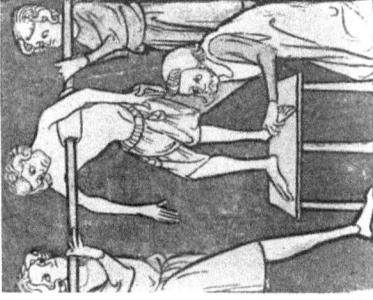

(C)

(B)

(A)

(E)

(D)

(A) BLEEDING A PATIENT [B.M. MS. Sloane 2435, 14c.]   (B) NURSES AND BED [V. & A. Mus. Facs. Psautier. Bib. Nat. Paris, 14c.]

(C) REDUCING DISLOCATED SHOULDER [B.M. MS. Sloane 1977, late 13c.]   (D) INTERIOR OF DOCTOR'S DISPENSARY. Full description in text

(E) EXTRACTING AN ARROW BY THE POINT [(D) & (E) Trin. C. Camb. MS. O. 1. 20, early 13c.

Medical and Scientific Folk

ROBES FOR A DOCTOR.
PATTERN of COSTUME

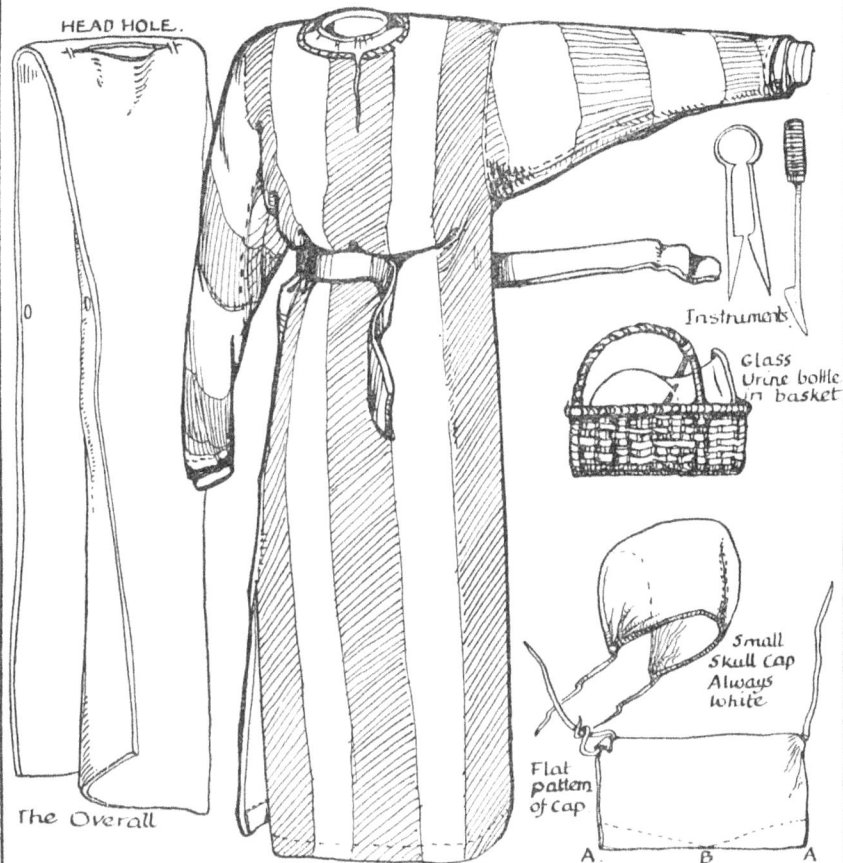

HEAD HOLE.

Instruments.

Glass
Urine bottle
in basket

Small
Skull Cap
Always
white

Flat
pattern
of cap

A.   B   A

The Overall

The Gown No. 1.

NO. 3

NO. 2

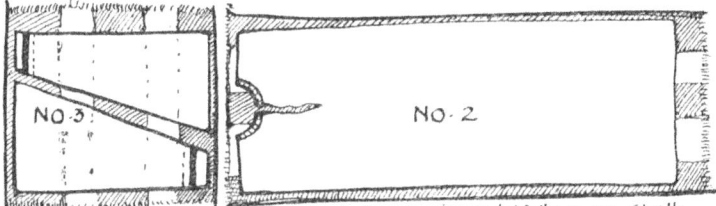

Sleeves on Cloth.

Back and Front pieces laid thus on Cloth.

century—The doctor lets blood, more usually an assistant holds the basin. Afterwards the wound is bound up and the doctor himself removes the cloths and blood. Note the surgeon's close linen coif, a head-dress in universal wear at that date, but from the latter part of the fourteenth century increasingly restricted to the professional classes, and eventually to the legal profession. The loose hanging sleeve of the patient has presumably been ripped at the shoulder for the occasion, but *cf.* the medico's upper gown or *garde-corps* in (D) and (E), slit on the upper arm to free the arm below, which in cold weather could be muffled in its ample folds. The close caps of these worthies recall the little Basque beret now popular for sport, even to the little stalk on top. (B) A modern-looking bed. Pillows were not as a rule in cases, but two squares of white linen knotted at the four corners covered them front and back. (See Beds, Interiors.) Patients naked, but head wrappings worn. (C) Reducing dislocated shoulder. See that implements are large size and well made. (One MS. shows an excellent Gotche's splint.) The drawers of the patient with gathered hem (see also (E)) are interesting, especially the way in which the ends of the legs are tied up to the waistbelt. Have everything well made and adequate. (C) and (E) are a warning to have the patient reasonably undressed before treatment. (D) Interior of a dispensary. On the shelves from left to right find bladders of lard, sponges, bags of seed, bundles of sticks, a horn of ointment, bundles of twigs and dried leaves, bunches of dried berries, rolls of bark and dried roots, round wooden basins and pots and animal skins stuffed full and hung up like bags. On the lower shelf strange shapes of jars and bottles from far countries. On the lower shelf rows of wooden boxes. Balances, pestle and mortar (a good action uses two hands, pestle in right and stirrer in left, a sort of double beating). A water bath on a tripod over the fire and a hooded fireplace. (E) Arrows are extracted by pushing through and pulling out the barbed head by its point. Bandages, modern style, slightly wider. Fluffed up flax and oily wool (creamy white) from the sheep's udder as a natural lanoline dressing. For crutches, etc. see p. 131 (' Invalids ').

THE WELL-TO-DO BURGHER

THE WELL-TO-DO MAN is suitably dressed in any of these opulent fur-lined coats (p. 27). The diagrams show their simplicity. Avoid worrying these clothes into a close fit by innumerable seams and darts. Spend longer on adjusting the shoulders and side seams so that the heavy material hangs well. To give the impression that the robe is very slightly on the large size is no fault. The mediæval people seem to enjoy a sense of lavish generosity in drapery. For this type of costume, get about twice as much stuff on to your figure as you would reasonably expect and you will be all right. Sleeves are set in plainly and have usually only one seam under the arm. Buttons may be polished wood, horn, metal, or covered with contrasting cloth, often matching the lining.

The coat (page 27, No. 2) is worn over a gown of the same material and fastened on the shoulder. The neck-band may be part of the under-robe. The cap is simple round felt, brightly coloured, with an edging of black curly lamb's wool (page 27, B, B^1). No. 1 has sleeves inset short and wide enough to show the gown below and split up the front for walking or riding. The cap (A^{11}) is most easily made, the circle of the crown being gathered around the back part only (A), and the whole eased into a straight band (A^1), which is rolled upwards to form the brim. Roll more tightly in front than behind to get the extra depth at the back of the head. The shoes (C and C^1) are the mediæval equivalent of elastic-sided slippers. The cloak (page 27, No. 3) is a straight piece of fur-lined cloth sewn plainly around the circumference of a circular cape. It is slipped on over the head, but keep the neck-opening as small as possible. It is better to line the top circle with strong unstretchable linen cloth rather than bulky fur. The hat at the bottom (page 27, No. 4) is made from pieces of shaped felt cut as shown (page 27, No. 5) and sewn up along the seams with bright cord. Two hats cut simultaneously from different coloured strips of felt gain a motley effect by using alternate pieces. Black and white lambskin would look very handsome.

ILLUSTRATIONS (p. 25 (A)).—A French model, *c.* 1430-40. Costumes akin to this are to be found in English MSS. and carvings. The gown (like its companion, p. 26 (C)) is of the *houppelande* type, so fashionable from the last years of the fourteenth century. The right arm uses the lower sleeve cuff, the left goes through a gap in the upper part of the sleeve seam. The 'topper' for summer wear was often of straw. (B) An early fourteenth-century illustration of the term 'cutpurse.' To avoid such *contretemps* the purse was often tied to a belt beneath the upper gown. Note the mail-clad *sergeant* with his mace of office, a forerunner of the modern police constable. (C) A street scene, *c.* 1455-60, shows the impartial fashion of short and long gowns side by side. Note the formal pleats fore and aft. The short cloak shown on the right-hand lower figure is not common. Also the long 'piked shoon' of the late fourteenth century have regained vogue after a brief loss of favour. The hood and chaperon are replaced by 'wide-awake' hats of felt or beaver. Both stalls are tables; the left a square one, the right three-legged circular. The stall effect is obtained by erecting a separate cover. Notice construction carefully. It could be unfolded and erected upon a stage or readjusted for screening purposes. The covering is of coarse material and can be roughly painted, as also the edges of the table or any sign-boards used.

N.B.—Use two or more thicknesses of wood; if using modern planks cut thin in the sawmill. Note the thickness of the table edge and shaping of the legs—with morticed struts so that the whole can be taken to pieces.

On page 26 (A), (B), (C) are from the same set of figures as page 25 (A). Although all belong to the second quarter of the fifteenth century (C) retains most of the features of the courtly wear of *c.* 1400. He wears a typical *chaperon* (see page 90), of which the liripipe has been unfortunately broken off (the end dangles from his hand). Page 26 (A) represents a prince in his robes of state; the hat here shown seems almost peculiar to the great. Page 26 (B) should be compared with the examples of ladies' rich attire on a later page. Page 26 (D) and (E) are Italian merchants of the middle and end of the fourteenth century, in dignified yet simple array. Note the close linen coifs and the little hoods arranged turban-wise.

(A)

(B)

(C)

(A) 'MAN ABOUT TOWN' (Coat has double hem described in text)
[Brass statuette by Jacques de Gerines, Rijks Mus., Amsterdam; Flemish, 15c. Casts in V. & A. Mus.]

(B) 'CUTPURSE' AND SERGEANT A STREET BY-PLAY
[B.M. Facs. 107, Gorleston Ps., early 14c.]

(C) STALLS BY THE GATE HOUSE, AN EXCELLENT MEDIÆVAL STREET SCENE
(Note the sound construction of stall, tables, etc.) [B.M. Facs. 233, 15c.]

(D)

(E)

(B)

(C)

A)

(A), (B), (C) Excellent Costume Studies
[Brass statuettes by Jacques de Gerines, Rijks Mus., Amsterdam ; Flemish, 15c.   Casts in V. & A. Mus,

(D), (E) Merchants and City Men [B.M. MS. Addl. 27695, 14c.]

COMFORTABLE ROBES FOR CITY MEN.

Pattern of Robe

NO. 1.

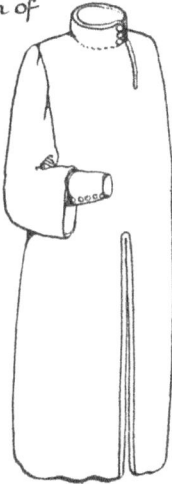

A

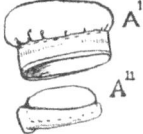
A¹

A¹¹

Pattern of Hat

Pattern of Robe.

No 2.

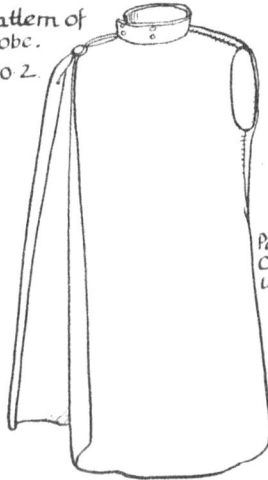

B

B¹

Pattern of Cap worn with robe.

C

C¹

Pattern of Shoe

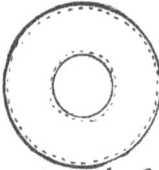

Pattern of Circular Cape
NO. 3.

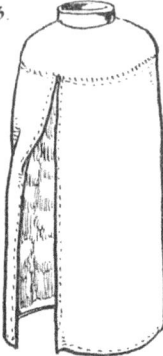

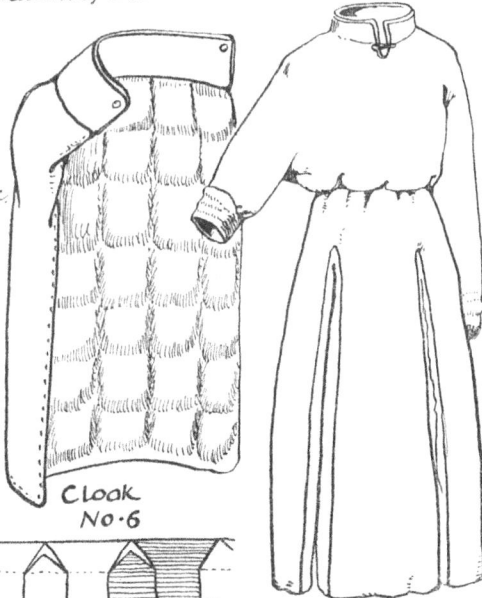

Cloak
No·6

Robe No·7

Hat pattern.
NO·4.

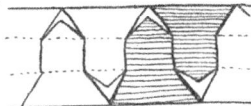

Pattern laid on Felt.
NO·5.

MUSICIANS

AFTER the careful restrictions of religion and royalty, musicians are refreshingly loose, and may wear anything. Since there is no definite costume for musicians we have concentrated on robes and sleeves that give free play to the arms.

The harpist (page 31, No. 2) is copied from a MS. where he wore a plain long gown of brown with comfortable fitting sleeves laced to fit the lower arm, under which you could see a loose white linen shirt, also with long sleeves. Over the brown robe was a loose white skin-lined cloak (page 31, No. 3) that could be fastened up the sides or held to the figure with a belt for warmth, but would swing clear and leave the arms free while playing. The string of the coif was loosed beneath his chin as he bent his head. The feet were in fur-lined slippers of dark cloth. The harp is as large as any in use and carried in a leather or thick felt case. The smaller harp on page 30 (B) was of a more usual size. The harp being tuned is a good shape and the key suggests a useful ' action.' A rabbit's skin or piece of cloth is frequently seen; used, we believe, to wipe the fingers before playing. The photograph costume is copied from a slightly earlier MS.; the usual plain woollen robe of natural coloured wool is worn over a linen slip with fitted sleeve—the loose outer sleeve could be thrown back when playing and the throat is free.

Unless for a very elaborate production the instruments shown on page 30 could be copied for show only, but many of the simpler instruments may be *used*. We have drawn a simple arrangement of bells (mindful of Christmas). We find these in the MS. hung overhead horizontally or perpendicularly; the arrangement needs no explanation save for the leather strap threaded behind the bells, which, slid forward by a movement of the foot, effectually mutes them all simultaneously (page 31, No. 4).

The lower part of the lantern may safely be made of wood; the lid and ring are metal (page 31, No. 1). Do not use clear glass; it cannot represent the thin horn of the original; but many non-inflammable substitutes may be found. The costumes of the musicians are simple, their instruments complicated beyond the scope of this book. Mediæval music seems to be a precious and difficult joy; make its exponents as comfortable as possible in the costume department.

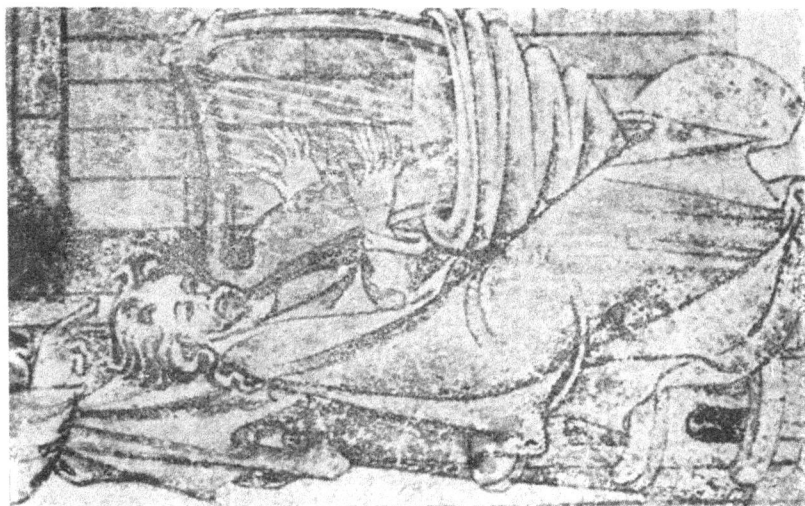

(B)

(A)

(A) A Harpist with a Large Harp still in its Covering Case of Leather or Thick Cloth

(The gown is made from the pattern on page 31, but the length in this case reaches to the ankles. The neck and sleeve edges are heavily worked with running stitches and the side pieces are pulled around almost to meet in front, giving the double skirted effect)

(B) The Original Picture [B.M. MS. Egerton 1894, 14c.]

(A)

(B)

(C)

(D)

(E)

(A) VARIOUS INSTRUMENTS [B.M. MS. Burney 275, 14c.]

(B) TUNING UP A SMALL HARP [B.M. MS. Addl. 28162, 13c.

(C) A PLAIN GOWN WITH BANDS OF COLOURED EMBROIDERY

(D) IN THE MS. THIS GOWN APPEARS TO BE GATHERED TO THE WAIST ON A RUNNING STRING THREADED THROUGH THE MATERIAL

[(C & D) B.M. Facs. 107, Gorleston Psalter, early 14c.

(E) LATER COSTUMES AND INTERESTING INSTRUMENTS, INCLUDING A DRUMMER BOY [Bodl. Liby. Ox. MS. 264, 14c.]

HARPIST'S ROBE

GOWNS FOR MUSICIANS.

Harp in Bag. No.2

Comfortable Cloak with adaptable Sleeve

Fur Cloak NO.3.

Under-robe

A Fur Wrap.

No.5

Bells. No.4.

Lantern. No.1

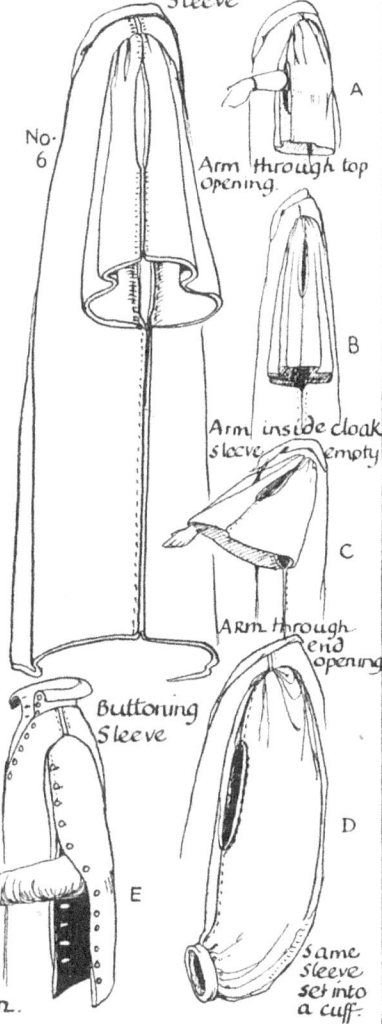

No. 6

A — Arm through top Opening.

B

Arm inside cloak sleeve empty

C

ARm through end opening

D

Buttoning Sleeve

E

Same sleeve set into a cuff.

HOSE AND BREECHES

To the casual enquirer it will no doubt seem a curious anomaly : it is none the less a fact that in the majority of costume-books no portions of man's apparel are slurred over in so haphazard a fashion as those under the above heading. Civilized custom agrees to regard them as indispensable : costume writers seem well-nigh to approach them as if they were (to use a ' genteel ' Victorianism) ' inexpressibles.' A few vague generalities, and casual references to Elizabethan ' trunkhose ' and Restoration ' petticoat breeches,' are as much as the public at large are permitted to know of the way in which our ancestors clothed their nether limbs—especially in the Middle Ages. The fact is our standard authorities have apparently but ill-defined notions of the essential meaning of such terms as ' breeches,' ' braies,' ' chausses,' ' hose,' ' trunkhose ' and the like, their application varying at hap-hazard, often from page to page. Regularly they confound the one with the other, irrespective of real changes that, in fact, *did* occur at successive dates. Fairholt's *Costume in England* is probably still, taking it all round, the best general handbook of the subject : yet many of his definitions, scattered *passim*, are as contradictory and misleading as any of the rest.

The point to realize at the outset is that ' hose ' (Fr. *chausses*, late Lat. *calcei, calceamenta* [1]) are primarily coverings for the legs (= stockings or leggings), whereas ' breeches ' (Fr. *braies*, Lat. *braccae*) are essentially coverings for the loins. The former, to be sure, may in process of time extend upwards till they unite at the fork and eventually reach to the waist ; the latter may at times reach down to the ankles. Moreover, since long, tight-fitting *braies* of coloured material seem at certain periods (notably eleventh and twelfth centuries) to have been favoured by the upper classes, there is sometimes a difficulty in determining from contemporary drawings and carvings which of the

[1] In *classical* Latin ' calceus ' stands for a closed half-boot or buskin, as opposed to the open sandal, ' calceamentum ' for footwear in general.

two is intended. The distinction is none the less a real one, and holds good (generally speaking) to the close of the Middle Ages. A few current errors should here be succinctly dismissed. *Chausses* and *hose* are identical in meaning, but one is a French (Anglo-Norman) and the other an English term. 'Breeches' is only a later form of O.E. *brec, brech, bryk*, etc. (Fr. *braies*, Lat. *braccae*), though the application of the term varies at different periods. 'Hose' was *not* (*pace* Fairholt and others) ' *originally* used to imply breeches *or chausses* ' (*sic*) : it is not so employed till the second half of the sixteenth century, *nor after* about the middle of the seventeenth. The Norman 'chausses' did not ' reach to the waist ' : hose of that type hardly occur before *c.* 1470. The use of the word ' trunkhose ' earlier than the sixteenth century is entirely out of place : both the word and the thing it denotes are wholly foreign to the Middle Ages,[1] with all due respect to Mr. Hilaire Belloc (' Joan of Arc '). One esteemed author speaks of ' loose braies *reaching up* to the knees ' and of ' braies or chausses ' as if synonymous. It is curious, by the way, that while in England the word ' hose ' reverted from mid-seventeenth century to its pristine sense of ' stocking,' in Germany it still retains its sixteenth-century meaning of ' breeches,' ' trousers.' It has seemed worth while to stress the foregoing points, since authorities as widely circulated as Gay, Quicherat, Racinet, Viollet-le-Duc and Hottenroth have had a large share in confusing the issues.

Note that women throughout the Middle Ages *never* wore breeches, but regularly wore *hose*, although the latter did not follow the successive changes undergone by their equivalents in male attire. From a relatively early date the breeches were generally accounted as the symbol *par excellence* of virility ; so much so as to constitute the whole point of more than one ribald *fabliau* of the times. Of a domineering wife it was a common saying : ' she wears the breeches.' The prosecution was careful to specify breeches (as well as *long* hose tied to the doublet) among the distinctively masculine items of apparel with which Joan of Arc was charged at her trial, although by that date they would normally have been concealed from view by the overlying doublet and hose.

Originally the breeches appear to have been cut on the lines of our pyjama-trousers, even to the method of securing them in position by a hem and running string at the waist. In common with the ancient Irish and Scots trews they seem at times to have fitted pretty closely

---

[1] The word does not seem to occur till the later Elizabethan age ; the *thing* first appears about the middle of the sixteenth century.

and been fitted with feet, and this it is no doubt that has helped to confuse them with the long hose of the later Middle Ages in the mind of many students.[1]   Where the nether-limbs were more or less exposed to view by current fashion, it seems early to have been generally felt that this loose trouser-form did less than justice to the line of ' a good leg ' and various devices were used from the ninth to the twelfth century to suggest the underlying shape.   Down to the latter date the ordinary tunic of everyday wear reached to the knee, so that only the leg proper (as opposed to the thigh) was regularly open to criticism.   ' Dressy ' men therefore tended either to shorten their breeches considerably or to cut them to fit the limbs as tightly as possible from the knee downward : in fact much like the Indian ' jodhpurs.'   Judging from contemporary illustrations (tenth to twelfth centuries) these close-fitting breeks were often accounted sufficient covering for the legs, but as often as not the lower leg is covered by close-fitting hose to the knee, on the lines of the old-fashioned ' hose ' of the Scots Highlands ; or the limbs were bound between ankle and knee either by diagonal crossbands or by a kind of ' puttees.'   The short hose (although shaped to the leg) for the most part show an obvious tendency to ' ruck ' ; commonly they have ornamented tops, and it seems far from certain that these do not form or conceal some sort of garter. For, in principle at least, there can be little doubt that garters are considerably more ancient than is commonly suggested in costume-books (*vide infra*).

[*Note.*—Hitherto the Bayeux Tapestry has been implicitly relied upon as firsthand contemporary evidence of the dress, arms, etc. of the Conquest.   It is therefore unfortunate—since we seem to have nothing to supply its place—that strong doubts have arisen as to its actual date of execution, varying by as much as 100 years.   If, as one school maintains, this document is no earlier than *c.* 1125, most of our traditional notions of costume in the latter half of the eleventh century must go by the board.   The question however remains an open one ; for those who would date the work within living memory of the events portrayed —say, roughly, 1090—have a strong case.]

With the twelfth century the hose increase and the breeches diminish in importance.   With the upper classes it is an age of long robes, whereby the legs are mostly concealed.   Only among the populace, especially rustics, were the old pyjama-trousers openly worn.

---

[1] The essential differences between *braies* and *chausses* and their respective evolution up to the late fifteenth century have been set forth in minute detail by A. Harmand : *Jeanne d'Arc* ; Paris, Leroux, 1929, pp. 73-97 and 123-145.

Alternatively the breeches worn by such at their work were a mere breech-clout (*see* pages 75, 78). We have, however, no lack of evidence as to the leg-wear of ' the better sort.' The breeches henceforth definitely become linen drawers, worn primarily for decency's sake, and no longer obtruded upon public notice. They are variously cut and adjusted to allow of the lower ends being caught up and attached by a string to the waistband or girdle. The short tunic to the knee was necessarily worn for action even by nobles, or (as a compromise) the long tunic was slit up in front (and behind ?) nearly to the fork. Where they are shown worn by men in vigorous motion or partly undressed, we get valuable revelations of the clothing of the lower limbs. The girdle-string of the breeches is commonly exposed at intervals : to it can be tied up the lower ends of the breeches, the hose, and various articles such as the purse, keys, etc. The hose now reach up to the thighs ; they fit with scarce a wrinkle to above the knees, whence they widen out so that the breeches can be tucked into them. In front they each rise to a sharp point to which is fastened a kind of bracing-cord attached to the breech-girdle. This method of fixing them is reminiscent of that now used for fishermen's ' waders.' Hose made more or less on these principles endured till far into the fourteenth century. As Miss Hartley rightly insists (p. 39), ' the hose are elongated stockings rather than breeches.' Their union at the top, whereby they become (in modern parlance) ' tights,' seems hardly to date much earlier than 1385-90. The nature of these ' elongated stockings ' will be better understood by reference to pages 33-37. Readers desirous of fuller particulars of their make may consult Harmand's *Jeanne d'Arc : Ses costumes, son armure*, pages 123-145. Practical experience vouches for the authenticity of the single seam down the back of the leg and for the ingenuity of the mediæval tailor, as shown by the alternate simplicity and complexity [1] of his patterns. The hose worn by all women of any standing were simply tailored stockings reaching to the knee or just above it and fixed by garters merely. Hence the charge brought against Joan of Arc by her judges of wearing ' long hose joined together and fastened by points to the gipon '—but that of course was at a later day. The long hose of the later twelfth century lasted without notable modification till about the middle of the fourteenth century, attached as before to the girdle-stead

---

[1] As an example of the latter we may cite the ' doublet of Charles of Blois ' (1364 ?) preserved in the museum at Lyons. It is composed of no less than *twenty-seven separate pieces*, all indispensable to give the characteristic bold outline, as modern experiments have proved.

in front.   Not infrequently a kind of button or knob was sewn to the top of each hose, to which the bracing-string or suspender was tied. From the close of the twelfth century the tendency grew to shorten the linen drawers or breeches (first to the knee, then to mid-thigh) and to reduce their width ; till, towards 1400, they attain the dimensions of our modern bathing-drawers or ' slips.'

With the adoption by the middle of the fourteenth century of shorter coats—gipons, cotehardies, doublets—the hose of the upper classes undergo a number of modifications.   They reach up, fore and aft, to the fork and fit throughout as skin-tight as cut and material can make them.   Henceforth they are no longer connected to the breeches (from now mere underwear and normally invisible), but to the doublet.   The latter during the third quarter, perhaps, of the century had a number of woven cords sewn to the lining inside in pairs which were passed through corresponding pairs of eyelet-holes set along the top of the hose all round.   By the last quarter of the century these ties are abandoned, both doublet and hose being perforated with eyelets at their overlap, through which the latter are tied to the former by *points* (=short, tagged laces).   At the same time the hose mount level with the hips, and by the close of the century are sewn together to form one garment—what we know as a ' pair of tights.'   With this new mode of leg-wear corresponds the introduction of the *codpiece*,[1] that bag-like pouch in front of the hose so conspicuous in the sixteenth century.   It is not, however, till the last quarter of the fifteenth that these ' tights ' ascend to the waist.   These successive alterations in the hose naturally entailed modifications in cut.   The old separate hose long survived side by side with the newer united form.   The smarter the hose the more numerous the points.   All action involving pronounced forward bending imposed considerable strain upon the hinder fastenings of the hose.   Hence labourers, artisans and in fact all men strenuously occupied would habitually undo the points at the back.   In execution scenes the headsman is nearly always thus shown.   The result is to reveal more or less of the underwear.   Even thus a modern man will commonly get him into his shirt sleeves to undertake a ' job of work.' In what respect (if any, apart from the tougher material) the ' arming hose ' worn under armour in the late fourteenth and fifteenth centuries differed is a question which seems hitherto to have attracted little or no attention.   It seems only reasonable to assume that in the field at least,

---

[1] In fact if not by name.   Most writers date it from the late fifteenth—or even the sixteenth—century.   Actually it appears as early as 1371 in a Vatican MS., ' Romaunt of the Rose.'

where the combatants' motions could not be limited by the cut and dried rules that governed the lists, the hose must have been designed to hamper action as little as possible.

With the advent of the Tudors we enter upon a new era in the evolution of the masculine nether garments. However interesting, the ensuing changes do not concern us here. A few remarks, however, seem desirable to round off our account of this portion of attire. As early as the twelfth century hose provided with (apparently) thin leather soles seem to have been in common use by the better class. These are regularly shown worn without other coverings for the feet; where shoes or boots are worn the hose are commonly made without feet, *i.e.* with no more than a loop or 'stirrup' of material passing under the instep. In most cases the *vampy* (covering for the instep and toes), soles and (very occasionally) the heels were each cut separately and sewn to the leggings. Less common were hose whose vampy was cut in one with the leg, while the sole was cut in one with 'clocks' or gores fitting in between heel and vampy over the ankle. The various fashions of toe found in mediæval boots and shoes are copied also in the leather-soled hose of the same date. Parti-coloured and otherwise variegated hose are not infrequent during the latter half of the fourteenth century and the early and late fifteenth century, often being the only portion of apparel thus diversified. Ordinarily, however, these are heraldic in origin, or denote a livery. Although mediæval accounts and inventories record hose of rich fabrics—silk and even velvet—it seems clear that the staple material in all classes was a loosely woven woollen cloth. Sometimes single, sometimes (in part at least) lined, they were all cut 'on the bias';[1] although the stuffs employed had a degree of elasticity unknown to modern drapers. Semi-tight hose or pantaloons of coarser stuff, often combined with gaiter-like wraps, distinguish rustics or the poorest classes.

F. M. K.

---

[1] References to the 'bias' of the hose repeatedly occur in old texts. Actual hose of the fourteenth century were excavated at Herjolfsnes (Greenland) in 1921.

GARTERS, SUSPENDERS, ETC.

WE referred a little further back to garters as opposed to cross-bands, puttees, suspenders and the like, and (p. 35) we saw that these were the usual support of the short hose of the ladies. Indeed, does not England's most noble order of chivalry traditionally owe its foundation (in 1348) to a lady's dropped garter? Be that as it may, the famous Luttrell Psalter, executed at most a decade earlier, unmistakably shows buckled garters, with hanging ends, worn below the knee by the male sex. In fact, in this MS. wherever the hose are revealed they show a band of decoration immediately under the knee; this also may likely enough represent a garter. Similar ornaments decorate the hose in more than one MS. of about 1200. Actual garters, with or without flying ends, are common enough in Carlovingian and Ottonian art (eighth-tenth centuries), where they confine the long *braies* at the knee and small of the leg. Except as part of the insignia of the Garter, however, nothing of the sort seems to have been in modish favour from mid-fourteenth to the sixteenth century.

Short puttee-like swathings (cf. p. 34) round the ankle and small of the leg occur in the twelfth century, often—if not generally—serving to hold in place the ' high-lows ' with which the wearers are shod. (In effect not unlike the example on page 93, No. 11.)

Some costume-writers, at a loss to explain the wrinkleless fit of mediæval-tailored hose (especially about the ankles), have suggested that actually they were made with an opening in the lower part, which in wear was either laced up or sewn together once in position. Exceptional examples of hose tied, laced or even buttoned up the small of the leg *can* be instanced; but that this was either necessary or usual is a gratuitous assumption (*see* note, page xiv).

SPORT

LONG-FITTING hose have always been a problem. Before making this diagram we consulted all possible authorities in hopes that someone had discovered a more perfect pattern, but though we found many specimens carefully measured up, the measurements were taken from a completed garment and are no guide for the first direct fitting, which must be done on the leg. For success, find a loosely woven cloth and use it cut on the cross. The pattern (page 43, No. 1) shows the shape of the completed piece very roughly; but do not attempt any cutting out even by the most careful measurements. You will only find the cloth pulls out of shape at once. Cut an oblong piece of cloth across into two triangular strips. Hold the centre of one of them to the centre front of the leg at the waist-line level and let it fall down over the instep. Slightly adjust top point to left or right till the front fold hangs straight down just touching the knee. Secure when the hang is right, tack around the ankle, and then, smoothing backwards from the front, work upwards, joining the seam up the back. The fit in the hose is got by taking every advantage of the elasticity of the material. When fitted, the surplus cloth is cut away. The back seam is strongly oversewn; use care, lest the stuff unravel. There will probably be some closely tacked material over on one side at the top of the back seam. This may be used to widen the seat of the breeches, but do not attempt any thing like a fitted top. If you look carefully at the workmen (page 63), you will see the hose are elongated stockings rather than breeches. At the top of the hose a few tactful pleats fit to the wearer's waist, where the hose are secured by ties to a fitted bodice. The undershirt being tucked into the top of the hose serves to make the skirt of the coat stand out more jauntily from the wearer's waist.

N.B.—Do not attempt to fit these hose into breeches, but fix the points that secure them to the bodice while actually on the wearer, that they may pull in the most convenient and comfortable places. Page 43, Nos. 2 and 3 display alternative ways of fitting the foot (or *vampy*) to the leg of the hose. Page 43 shows (No. 4) the hunting coat with very modern shoulder gussets: very effective when they show an under-shirt of the same colour as the hose, and (No. 5) a hawking glove of thick leather with a strengthened wrist; above is a hood for the hawk. Page 43 (No. 6) shows a gay woollen tassel over a wooden knob to which is fastened a piece of meat; this is the lure to which the hawk turns.

MS. ILLUSTRATIONS.—Sport, page 42. Do not confuse these sporting people with the common foresters and hunting folk of *fabliaux* and *fairy tales*. Their tight hose and short coats are more like those worn by the dandies in Court and about town. The long hose worn by the poorer sort were made from very coarse cloth and fitted far less neatly; often it had binding wrapped over it to hold it to the leg. All these illustrations date from the later fifteenth century, and the hose unite at the top to form tights; in (A) the points are untied wholly or partly and one wrestler shows the codpiece.

Three Aspects of Hawking Costume founded on page 42 (B)

(A)

(B)

(C)

(D)

(A) Youths Exercising : Wrestling and Quarter Staff [Essenwein, *Mediæval Housebook*, 15c.]

The quarter staff was 6-8 feet long, of ash or oak. It was swung around into definite ' guards ' and ' passes '

(B) Hawking Costume. See pages 35 and 37 [B.M. MS. Addl. 18852, 15c.]

(C) Short Coat and Hose [B.M. MS. Addl. 24098, 15c.]

(D) Scene for Sports Garden, Archery, Butts and Pavilions, etc.

[Bodl. Liby. Ox., Douce MS. 193]

HUNTING & HAWKING COSTUME

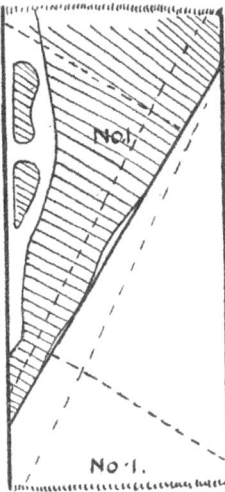

Cloth for the hose in position against the wearer's leg.

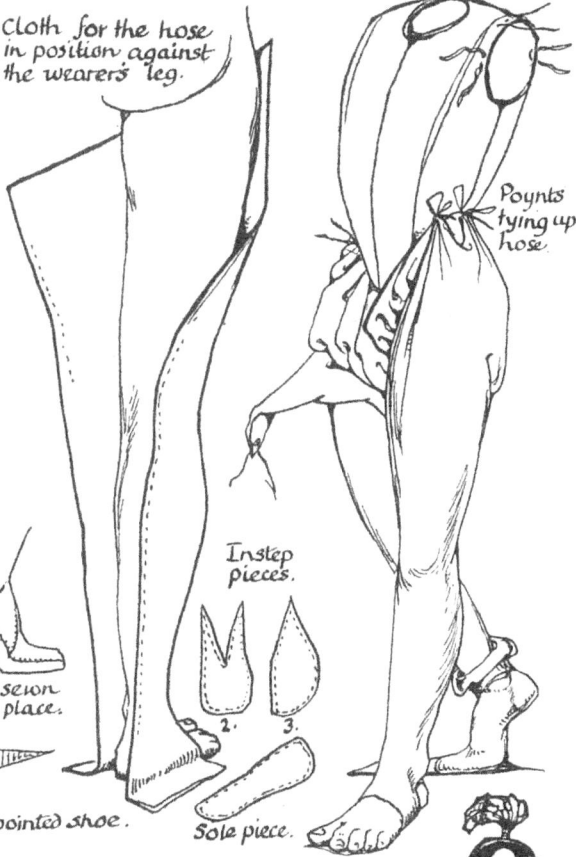

No.1

No.1.

Poynts tying up hose.

No.2 No.3

Two instep pieces.

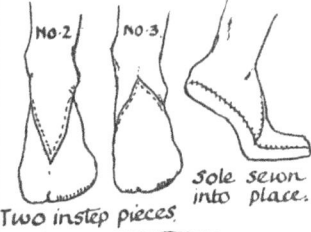

Sole sewn into place.

Instep pieces.

2. 3.

Sole piece for Long pointed shoe.

Sole piece.

gussets

No.4

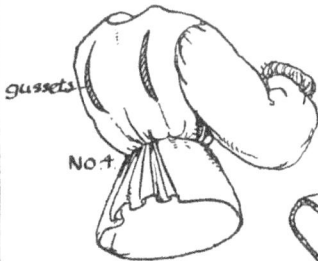

Leather Sporting Jerkin with inset shoulder gussets.

Hawks Hood.

Hawking glove. No.5.

Hooded Hawk.

Woollen tassle or Lure. No.6.

KNIGHTS AND ARMOUR

Arms, both offensive and defensive, played too important a rôle in the Middle Ages to be briefly dismissed in any work purporting to give even a summary of the externals of life during that era. In principle at least religion and chivalry were regarded as the twin ideals of Christian endeavour, and the knight who consistently lived up to the theoretical rules of his order—the ' very perfect gentle knight '—was, not unjustly, accounted the most accomplished type of layman. As such the heroes of history and legend provided literature and art with an inexhaustible fund of themes, second only to that ever available in the Scriptures and the lives of God's saints.

Of course there can be no question here of retracing for the thousandth time the evolution of arms and armour. There is no dearth of treatises, monographs and manuals devoted to the subject in general and in detail.[1] There are, however, a number of points worth discussing as to the actual nature of the armour worn and its practical adaptability to use, which are apt to be ignored or slurred over in most books. Almost inevitably, in doing so, something more than a hint of the evolutionary process must needs emerge in the course of these remarks. As is very pertinently pointed out elsewhere (see *Knights*, page 53), ' knights '—or indeed soldiers generally—did not normally go about the more humdrum business of life ' armed at all points.' The popular idea of the mediæval ' knight ' as a man who spent most of his waking hours locked from top to toe in shining steel is a mere Wardour Street myth. Even the heaviest-armed cavalry—the ' men at arms '[2] as they were termed from the fifteenth century—only wore

[1] An exceptionally full bibliography of the subject by F. H. Cripps Day is appended to vol. v. of Laking's *Record of European Armour.*

[2] No ' mediæval ' term has been or is more misused than this. Some of our best writers habitually employ it of (*a*) an armed retainer or guard in general, or (*b*) a common soldier, mounted or on foot, apparently as distinguished from a ' knight.' Actually the term seems to date from the establishment, under Charles

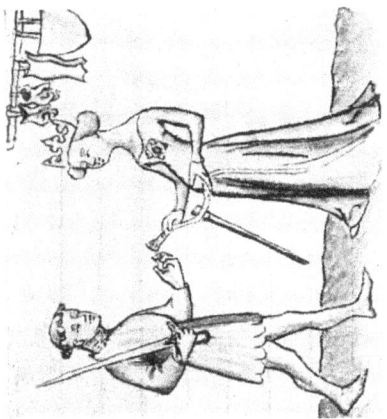

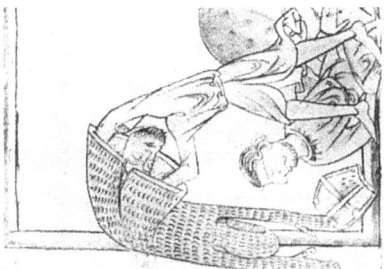

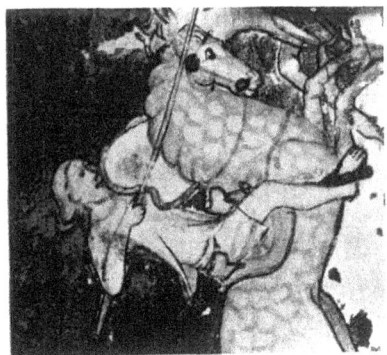

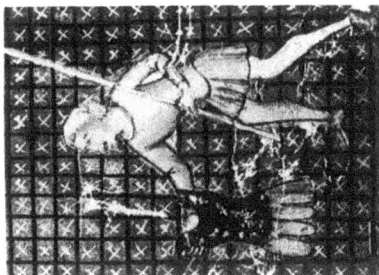

(A) SHIRT AND SHORTS

(B) A PLAIN SLIT SHIRT, WORN UNDER THE CHAIN MAIL, POSSIBLY IN CHAMOIS LEATHER [Trin. C. Camb. MS. O. 9. 34, mid. 13c.]

(C) THE SWORD BELT [B.M. MS. Addl. 38120, 14c.] After handing the knight his sword, the damsel buckles on his belt

(D), (E), (F) ARE OTHER STUDIES OF KNIGHTS THAT MAY HELP THE COSTUMIER [(A), (D)-(F) B.M. MS. Addl. 12228, 14c.]

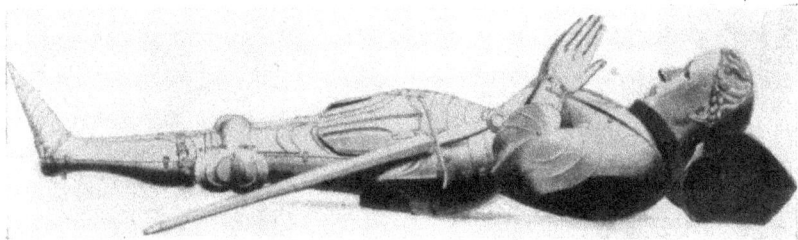

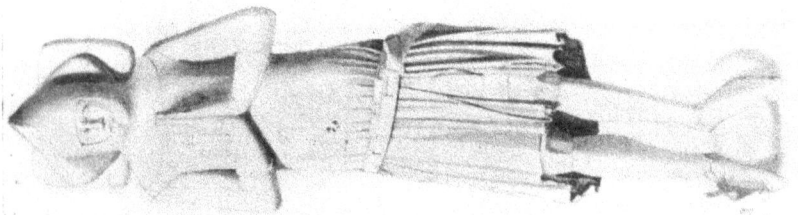

FOURTEENTH CENTURY AND LATER EFFIGIES OF KNIGHTS

(A) SIR ROBERT DU BOIS, 1311, FERSFIELD, NORFOLK [C. Stothard, dt.]

(B) MAILED EFFIGY AT CASTLE ASHBY, NORTHANTS.

(C) BRONZE EFFIGY OF RICHARD BEAUCHAMP, EARL OF WARWICK, IN ST. MARY'S, WARWICK, EXECUTED 1450–54 [C. Stothard, dt.]

(D) ROBERT, THIRD BARON WILLOUGHBY, AND LADY NEVILLE, A.D. 1380, SPILSBY, LINCS.

cap à pié armour on special occasions or when immediate fighting was expected ; in fact the helmet and gauntlets were rarely donned except on the very point of charging into action.   Armour at best was never *comfortable*, and only cowardice or childish vanity can normally have induced a man to encase himself wholly in a steel shell for any longer than mere expediency dictated.   Even when fully armed the only distinguishing marks of a knight, *as such*, were his gilt spurs, his heraldic crest and bearings and the insignia of some particular order of knighthood.   Remote from the field or the lists, he would as a rule dress in accordance with his social rank so far as his means allowed.   Contrary to ' romantic ' conceptions, gentlemen *previous to the sixteenth century* did not normally wear swords.   The only weapon that is generally in evidence—from the early fourteenth century onward—with civilian apparel is the dagger.   In an unruly and imperfectly policed age, the authorities, ever suspicious of armed risings, sternly discouraged the bearing of other lethal weapons by all classes, without valid reasons. Thus, in troubled times, travellers might carry a sword or other arm against emergencies on the road.

Although the ' common sort,' and probably too the poorer gentry, doubtless had to make shift, to some extent, with defences of canvas or leather padded and/or reinforced more or less with pieces of metal, there can be little doubt that from an early date those who could come by it were armed in mail—' chain-mail ' to use a pleonasm in generally accepted use—*i.e.* a network of interlinked rings.[1]   How *widely* it was patronized is an open question : its antiquity, ubiquity and continuity as a defence among European nations can be established beyond peradventure.   Scale armour was also used from a remote date and on the evidence it seems safe to assume that some form of ' plate ' armour was introduced earlier than is commonly assumed.   Both mail and (later) ' plate ' necessitated the use of special underwear—acktons, gambesons, arming doublets and arming hose—of leather or stout canvas, padded and quilted to protect the wearer from serious

VII of France, of the *compagnies d'ordonnance* as the nucleus of a standing army. The main strength of this was the ' man at arms ' or *homme d'armes* (pl. *gens d'armes* ; hence *gendarme*, a term which survives in France exclusively to denote a member of the *military* police) : the horseman armed from head to foot in heavy plates.   The term ' knight ' denotes purely a definite military caste, with special privileges.   In feudal armies the heavy cavalry were the *élite* ; but by no means every knight could afford or chose to serve among them.

[1] The extension of the term *mail* to any other type of armour is an error mainly due to *late* poetical licence and the ill-founded theories of early antiquaries, notably Meyrick.

contusions. Such clothes, however, would usually be changed once the necessity for resuming armour became remote. It must be remembered, on the other hand, that the donning and adjustment of the complete fighting-kit, even with every item laid in readiness and help at hand, took from first to last a good deal of time, nor was the task of disarming much easier. And yet I have read a story of a fugitive, with the hunt at his very heels, baffling the pursuers by concealing himself unaided at a moment's notice in one of the panoplies in the ' ancestral ' armoury ! Not time only but practice was required for the proper adjustment of the numerous ties, buckles and catches which held the equipment in position. Neither arming nor disarming was a thing to be undertaken for a mere whim. The technical history of armour and weapons in England prior to Tudor days remains hitherto unwritten. That many of the finest examples were imported seems clearly demonstrated, but what of the home-made article ? The evidence of monumental effigies and brasses seems to show that the panoply of the English knight, whether of native or foreign make, had a character of its own that need not fear comparison with Continental work. In the general lines of its evolution the armourer's art in England would seem closely to have followed the French and Flemish models rather than the example of Germany or Italy. Nor indeed do the dates of the principal modifications of form vary much between the respective nations. In fact, from more or less continuous political contact throughout the centuries, a certain amount of give and take would not seem an unfair inference.

Not till far into the twelfth century was armour (of mail) protecting the wearer ' at all points ' evolved. But the chief drawback of mail was the amount of underpadding entailed. However impenetrable to point or edge, the pliant links were only too apt to be driven into the flesh beneath and the subcutaneous bones—patella, shin, elbow, clavicle—to be cracked within their covering. Hence the gradual overlaying of the mail by plates of iron, latten or specially hardened and moulded leather that began with the second half of the thirteenth century and culminated in the complete armour of plate or ' white harness ' produced about 1400. Especially cumbrous must have been the knightly equipment of the time of Edward III, consisting as it did of superimposed layers of (1) padding, (2) mail, and (3) plate ; quite apart from the special underwear, the universal heraldic ' coat-armour ' and helm, the shield, sword, dagger, etc., attached to the fighter's person. In the fifteenth century the mail had been reduced to pieces attached to the arming doublet and hose at most of the points exposed by the harness of plate. In fact, what is commonly described as ' Gothic armour ' combines a minimum of weight with a maximum of resistance *and* freedom of action such as was achieved at no period before or since. In fact it has been found, I understand, from personal experience, that a perfectly made ' Gothic ' suit *can* at a pinch be worn and moved in without undue strain for considerable periods together.

Need we say that during the whole of the Middle Ages the armour of the rank and file of the troops, the men of the feudal and local levies, was far lighter and less complete ? Mobility was essential to them, while to the heavy-armed knight mounted on a ' great horse,' often armed likewise, weight was a tactical necessity in the charge : he might in a measure be compared to a ' tank.' Although a few examples are known of Italian suits (designed for fighting on foot in the lists) of the sixteenth century, where the soles of the feet alone are un-protected by steel plates, the completest war-harness of the ' Gothic ' era did not hermetically encase its wearer. In practice certain gaps proved inevitable : notably the back of the thigh (more or less pro-tected when in the saddle, where a rigid metal shell would have rendered the seat impossible), the ham, fork, and arm-pit. Various devices were employed to render most of these points less vulnerable.

Gothic armour relied for its efficiency not on its toughness alone, but to a marked degree on the skill with which its planes were designed to deflect impinging weapons, so that any but a direct hit would glance off and spend its force on the air. From the close of the fourteenth century, with the development of the hammerman's art, the heavy cavalry came in general to dispense with the protection of the shield. The mounted knight had manœuvred to encounter his ' opposite ' shield to shield, *i.e.* left side to left, the offensive rôle devolving wholly on the right hand. Now the ' knightly ' harness was of stouter metal and more massive design on the left (or more exposed) side, which was often further protected by ' double pieces ' or ' pieces of advantage,' *i.e.* extra plates or reinforcements, mobility being sacrificed to security.

A padded cap was worn under the mail hood and the various helmets were ingeniously lined, from an early date, so as to isolate the head from contact with the metal walls.

Although authentic armour *of the Middle Ages* (outside of a few world-famous collections) is of the greatest rarity nowadays, especially in England, no country in all the world is richer than ours in monu-mental effigies and brasses, providing an unrivalled series of models of the military equipment of the knightly warrior from the thirteenth century onward. Some idea of our wealth of sepulchral memorials may be gained from a perusal of the admirable works devoted to the subject, from Stothard and Hollis down to Prior and Gardner and Crossley. Boutell, Haines and others have specialized in the study of brasses. Excellent though most of these are, they give but an imperfect idea of *the mere quantity* of such monuments still extant throughout the length and breadth of the land. Hardly an outlying village church but can furnish an example, not seldom in remarkable preservation. That this should be so is amazing, in view of the iconoclastic fanaticism of the sixteenth-seventeenth centuries, the ' aesthetic ' hostility of the eighteenth, and the indifference of later incumbents. Injudicious ' restoration ' in the nineteenth century must also be borne in mind. Individual enthusiasts and historical commissions have done and are doing much to familiarize us with these ' Gothic ' masterpieces. It must however be remembered that ' measured drawings ' and half-tone reproductions from photographs, however good, can never be more than indifferent substitutes for intelligent personal inspection, and that that cardinal rule of textual criticism—' always verify your authorities *at first hand* '—applies equally here. Especially nowadays, when the motor is daily increasing the accessibility of everything, our opportunities in this way are limitless. The amount of detailed information which a single well-preserved effigy will often supply as to the construction and adjustment of armour is worth half the handbooks on the market.

If you care for these records of the past and are fortunate enough to have some slight artistic skill, you will be well advised to carry a notebook and pencil with you upon your jaunts. Whether motoring or ' hiking,' what more pleasant objective could there be than one of our glorious cathedrals or beautiful old parish churches ? Note, too, that the ' setting ' of these shrines is almost invariably picturesque, so that the pilgrim's way is apt to be a revelation of an England that persists in remaining lovely in despite of industrial ' progress.' To your non-antiquarian companions the mere delight of the journey will, as often as not, prove its own reward.

F. M. K.

(E)

(F)

(G)

(H)

ENGLISH EFFIGIES OF KNIGHTS

(E) EFFIGY IN FREESTONE, A.D. 1310, THRECKINGHAM, LINCS.
(F) WOODEN EFFIGY, ABOUT A.D. 1300, ABERGAVENNY, MON.
(G) FREESTONE EFFIGY OF A HASTINGS, A.D. 1348, ABERGAVENNY, MON.
(H) EFFIGIES, MONTGOMERY, WALES [late 14c. (further figure) and late 15c. (nearer)

NOTES ON ILLUSTRATIONS OF KNIGHTS

Page 45 (B). A knight donning a hauberk of mail. Note the attached hood and gloves; also the characteristic close helm of the period (mid-thirteenth century) with breathing holes (on ground to left).

(E) Arming knights (late fourteenth century). Note the great war-helm being put on one man [1]; another slips his coat armour over what suggests a primitive cuirass.

Pages 46 and 51. (B), (E) and (F) are good examples of mail of the late thirteenth to early fourteenth centuries. Note in (A) the curious leather gauntlets, the plate (or cuirbouly) knee guards and the tall open helmet (bascinet). (G) (mid-fourteenth century) and (D) (beginning of fifteenth) illustrate the gradual development of plate armour till in (C) we have the finished product as turned out by a great master. This last is the latten effigy in the Beauchamp chapel, Warwick, of Richard Beauchamp, earl of Warwick (†1439 at Rouen), and the figure is of special interest, as the model for the armour is obviously a work of the great Milanese workshops of the Missaglias. Specially interesting in (H) is the contrast between the late fourteenth century and the close of the fifteenth.

KNIGHTS

PERHAPS the amateur has more difficulty with his knights in armour than any other of the historical figures he desires upon his stage. Armour itself is beyond the scope of the amateur. If he can get well-fitting armour to suit the date he requires, he may use it. Otherwise, it is much better boldly to arrange some plain conventional substitute that will convey the sense of a solid grey mass of steel and give a uniform to your ranks. It is much better to say boldly, these are armed men—this is an army, than to have inaccurate tin contraptions.

[1] Apparently on to the bare head, which is, to say the least, very irregular.

Chain mail can more easily be managed by the amateur, and the coverings (surcoats, etc.) make many representations possible. But these coverings themselves are a pitfall, for they must hang over armour and you will not get the effect by slinging drapery over the figure to hide the armour which isn't there. Also, and this is a point often overlooked, the shining armour during warfare or on lonely journeys was frequently such a mass of thick grease and lamp-black that it looked like a camp kitchen. Luckily, the times when knights wore full armour were comparatively rare and the amateur will do well to study the knight's appearance under household circumstances or in tents or council chambers, where his dress was less impressive and is much easier to copy. Frequently your knight wore a close-fitting complete suit of chamois leather or, we believe, of linen-lined thick cloth. This with comfortable slippers and a cloak must often have been his appearance directly after the squires had removed his heavy armour. The knight on horseback (page 45 (A)) shows a good arrangement of shirt and breeches, and the one wriggling into his mail (page 45 (B)) shows another possibility. Leather armour is frequently possible, damped and shaped to the figure and painted and polished when desired. Be sure the heraldry of any known family is perfectly correct and be sure you copy your knights with very great understanding of their qualifications.

HUNTING

THE MS. from which the photo is copied (*Queen Mary's Psalter*) shows the commonest form of mediæval costume (page 57, No. 1). Variations of this costume clothe most of the hurried earnest little figures in the earliest MS. For most ordinary jobs and poor wearers you can be fairly safe to use some form of this shirt. To cut: measure the wearer over the shoulder from the knee in front to the back of the knee and cut this length generously twice in narrow cloth ; or once in wide cloth (the diagram is for narrow cloth). Lay flat and add on either side an extra length of material. Leave the neck-opening and slip the whole on to the figure. Raise the arms to shoulder level and mark where the natural waist comes across the side pieces. Take off and lay flat again. Cut through the side pieces at the waist-line. The top portion is then seamed up to form the sleeve and secured down an inch or two of the sides. The lower back pieces hang loose and widen the skirt. The diagram should make this clear. The extra front pieces may be left on and worn tucked backwards. But they are better detached : when a useful hood can be made from them. The garment is now made. To wear it, slip it on over the head with the side flaps falling loose. Pass the belt behind the back and ease the fulness around the waist. Let the side flaps be folded forward and upwards on either side—the belt is then fastened. The whole secret lies in adjusting the folds. When wrapping over the back pieces, bend the knees upwards and outwards so that the front portion is slightly eased forward, giving freedom of movement in front. To allow freedom in bending, pull the rear portion towards the centre of the back to give bending freedom, and the side pieces should be pulled upwards and forwards under the belt till the folds hang comfortably. With a little practice this simple shirt, properly adjusted, gives perfect ease and freedom of movement. In wear the legs seem to shake the folds into easy position. On slender figures the garment is apt to drag when the arm is raised over the head, because the side pieces fall

(A)

(B)

(A) & (B)   A Gown copied from Pattern on page 57
    It is very simple and permits of variations in wear and accessories

(A) [B.M. Roy. MS. 2 B. vii, 14c.]

         The hood also is shown on page 57.

(A)

(B)

(C)

(D)

(A) DAVID [B.M. Facs. 107, Gorleston Psalter, early 14c.]

(B) ARCHERS, FATHER AND SON. ONE SINGLE ROBE EACH (page 57)
(The small boy also wears footless hose, probably tied up to the waist)
[B.M. MS. Egerton, 1894, 14c.]

(C) AN EARLY PICTURE SHOWING THE EFFECTIVE USE OF A CHECK ON AN EXTREMELY SIMPLE PATTERN [B.M. Roy. MS. 12. C. XIX, 12c.]

(D) A FIFTEENTH-CENTURY BOAR HUNT, IN HOSE, DOUBLET AND LEATHER BOOTS
[B.M. Facs. 182]

HUNTING COSTUME

A well slung horn. NO. 4.

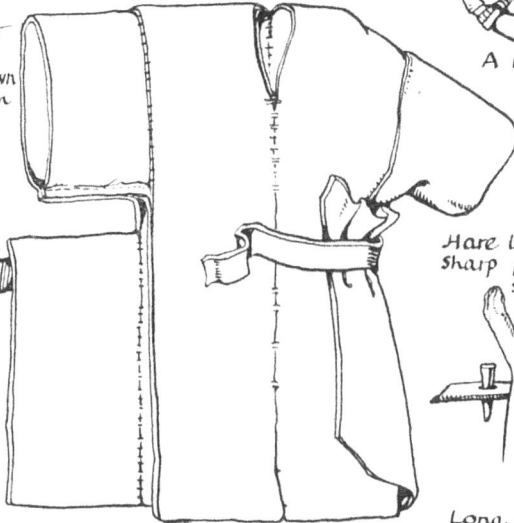

Top part of side width sewn up to form sleeve.

Belt.

Loose side-piece.

Hare legs on sharp pointed stick. NO. 5.

The make-up of the mediaeval robe. NO. 1.

Long, thick English bow. No. 3.

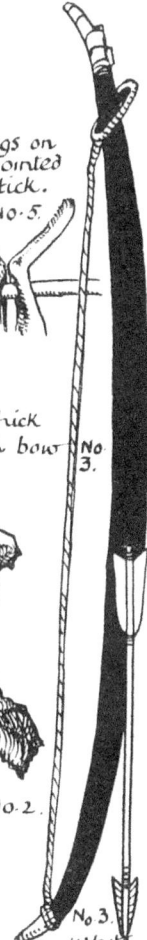

Head-piece

neck-piece.

Fur-hood. No. 2.

How to cut two fur hoods out of one skin so arranged, that the fur falls away from the face, and downwards from the neck-join.

No. 3. white feathered arrow

too far down the upper arm. To remedy, take a large pleat down the centre back and front seam to the top of the neck-split. This brings the armhole closer to the figure and the whole sleeve should fall inwards and leave the raised arm bare.

THE FUR HOOD (p. 57).—There is no adequate substitute for real fur. Page 57, No. 2, shows how two hoods may be cut from one large skin so that—a vital point—the fur falls back from the face and down from the neck-join.

Bow (page 57).—This is shown to ensure its being made thicker than modern ones. Strong stage lighting can cause a slender bow to become almost invisible and look feebly inadequate. The ends or notches are made of sheep's horns, the arrows heavily plumed with white goose-feathers (page 57, No. 3).

(Page 57, No. 4).—A hunting horn should be slung carefully or it will bump about. Scrape a groove around the horn or shrink a woollen cord on to it for a firm grip around the sloping surface.

HINTS. (Page 57, No. 5).—A simple way of collecting game on to a sharp pointed stick without fumbling with bits of string.

HUNTING—ILLUSTRATIONS

(Page 56)—(D), *c.* 1460.—Noble in hunting dress. Note the long boots with coloured turnover tops. Note the boar-spear with its characteristic cross-bar. This prevents the spear from being engaged too deeply, and also helped to hold the wounded beast at a distance.

ARTISANS

THE craftsman must never be confused with the labourer. If you have an artisan to dress, first find out what you can about the trade-guilds, the privileges and tools of your subject, and his position as apprentice, journeyman, maker of a masterpiece, or past-master. Craftsmen worked collectively and individually. The worker engaged 'on his own' upon a particular job existed in those days as always. The MSS. show many varied costumes for many varied trades. Some may be made after the pattern on page 73, some by that on page 83, and we give in pattern (page 61) another form having double-strength shoulders. This curious pattern is more easily made up than described. It will be seen in the fitting to be the basis of some otherwise puzzling shoulder-cape forms. It would be very suitable for heavy trades that have much carrying or shoulder work to do. The flat pattern (page 61, No. 1) shows the front and back pieces, with the neck and shoulder cuts marked. To make the shoulder seam, the front and back pieces are overlapped rather more than the height of the neck-piece left between them. The raised neck-band is thus formed by the front and back centre pieces of the coat. The side seams and front darts up the collar-band allow for close fitting to the neck. The shoulder seams may be stitched down plainly or shaped as on page 61, No. 2. The shoulder pieces are elongated into cape-shaped straps; the comfort of this (page 61, No. 3), for the pack-carrier (page 61, No. 4), will be seen at a glance.

For anyone carrying a pole on his shoulder a little padding, inserted on the shoulder between the double thickness, will be a great comfort. And it won't slip about.

The light wooden frame (page 61, No. 5) was used for carrying glass, and could be used for anything similar. Page 61, No. 4, is a tinker with bellows and hand-forge complete; an effective figure in a crowd. The apron (page 61, No. 6) is made from one skin, the naturally thick neck-piece making a useful pocket for the tools. A tool-bag similar to those in use to-day is shown (page 61, No. 7) ; the original was leather and rope, but basket-straw lined with cloth was probably used also. The coat (page 61, No. 8) is that worn by the boy in the photo under his leather apron. For his cloth hose, see pages 39 ff. ; his cap (page 61, No. 9) is made like a modern tam-o'-shanter. The whole round top and the under circle are sewn together around the rim ; turned inside out ; and fastened down on to the deep band, which goes two-thirds round the back of the head. This band is sometimes turned up jauntily, so that it looks rather like a circular pie-dish, or sometimes flapped down over the ears.

The workman here (page 65) has rolled down one of his dark hose. It may have been he had broken his points on that side, or he may be going to roll down the other leg as soon as he can spare time from burning the martyrs. The only slight alteration in the photograph based on this costume are the shoes, which in the original were natural coloured leather. The top head-wrap was a piece left over from making the hose. It is a plain square, the front edge of one side binding the forehead and the corners twisting as they pass back above the ears to tie behind the head. See that these corners are well twisted so as to form a circular roll that goes round the head.

ARTISANS—ILLUSTRATIONS

Page 63 (B).—Note the turban-arrangement of the hood, also the long ' piked ' toes and the strapped-on clogs, late fifteenth century.

(C).—Late fifteenth century. Note the diversity of hats and caps, also varied length of tunics. One man wears a hat over a close hood and loose leggings tied over hose. Another wears a coif or caul. Aprons are well shown.

Page 65 shows the hood twisted into a head-wrap, and close half-boots. One leg of the (separate) hose is turned down below the knee, where the tight-rolled top forms a garter.

Page 67.—Left-hand figure in linen coif and shirt (at side a glimpse of drawers (breeches), hose unbraced. Centre figure in shirt, down-turned hose and shoes, hair confined by a strip of linen. The bare-legged man on right has put his head through the face-opening of his hood ; note gorget and liripipe projecting fore and aft.

A GOOD PATTERN FOR WORKERS.

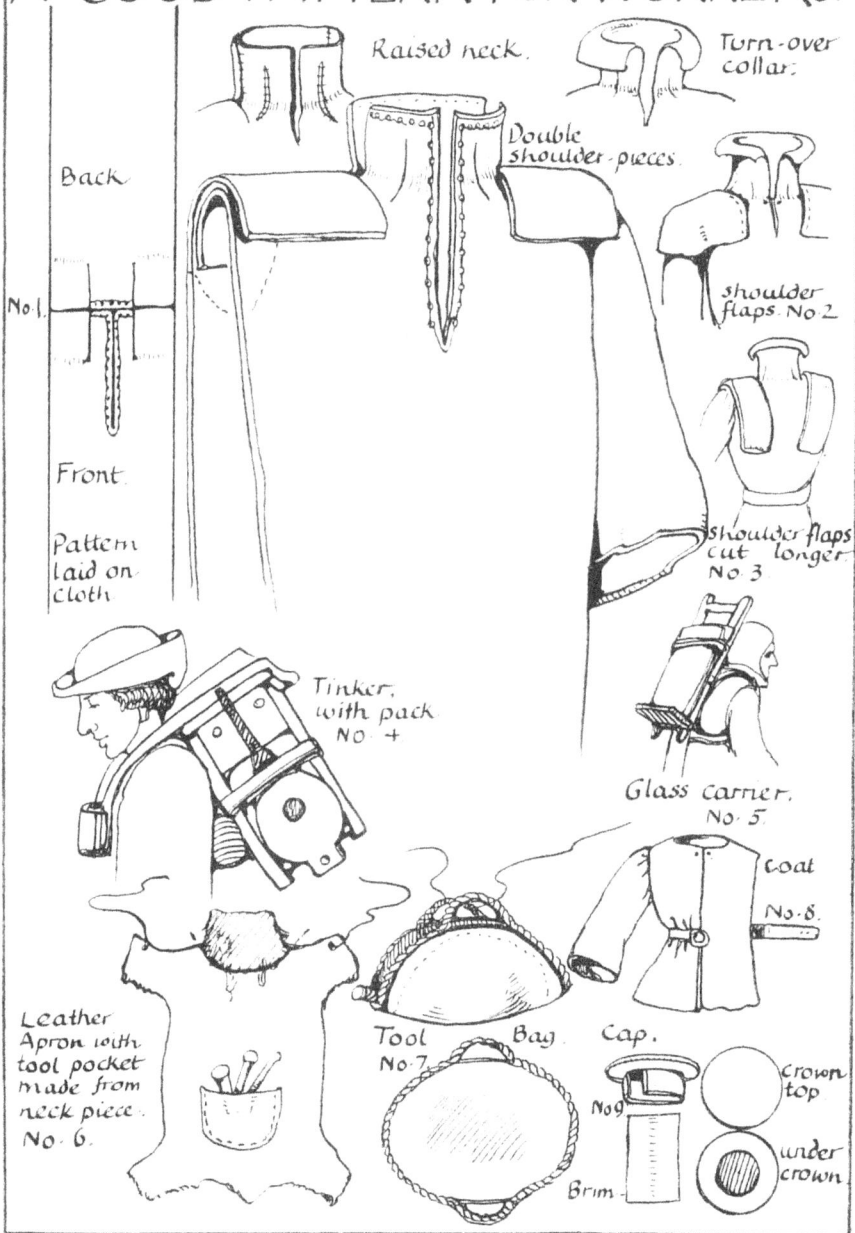

Raised neck.

Turn-over collar.

Back

No.1.

Front.

Pattern laid on cloth

Double shoulder-pieces.

shoulder flaps. No 2

shoulder flaps cut longer No. 3

Tinker, with pack No. 4

Glass carrier. No. 5.

Coat No. 8.

Leather Apron with tool pocket made from neck piece. No. 6.

Tool Bag No. 7.

Cap. No 9

Crown top

under crown

Brim.

Coat made from Pattern upon Page 61, but with Open Neck and Loose Linen Shirt showing at Neck and Wrist. Hose (page 43) and Cap (page 61). Leather Apron (see Apron Wearers, p. 73)

(A)   (B)

(C)

(A)   Two Men building a Wattle Fencing : Tight Coats belted at Waist, Hose and
      Socks and Shoes   [B.M. MS. Addl. 19720, 15c.]

(B)   A Clever Old Metal Worker
      (Notice the spectacles and clogs and old fur-lined coat.   An excellent costume to copy)
                                          [Essenwein, *Mediæval Housebook*, 15c.]

(C)   Various Trades have equally Varied Costumes   [B.M. MS. Addl. 18750, 15c.]

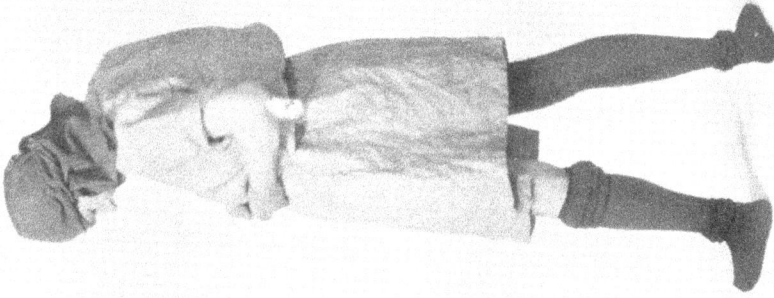

(B)

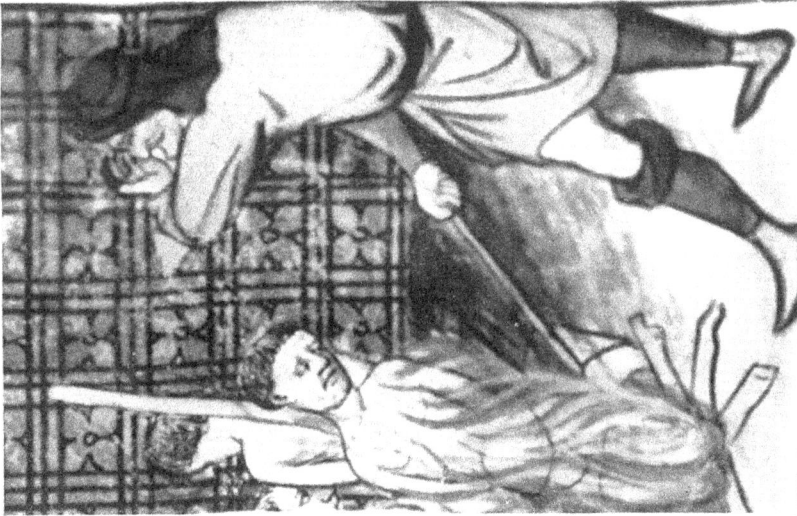

(A)

(A) & (B) PERHAPS THE MOST GENERALLY USEFUL COSTUME IN THE BOOK. COAT GOWN (page 57). HOSE (page 43). HEAD-WRAP A SINGLE PIECE OF CLOTH. SOFT LEATHER FOOT-SHAPED BOOTS WITH SOCKS ROLLED DOWN OVER THE TOPS [(A), B.M. Roy. MS. 20. C. VII. 14c.]

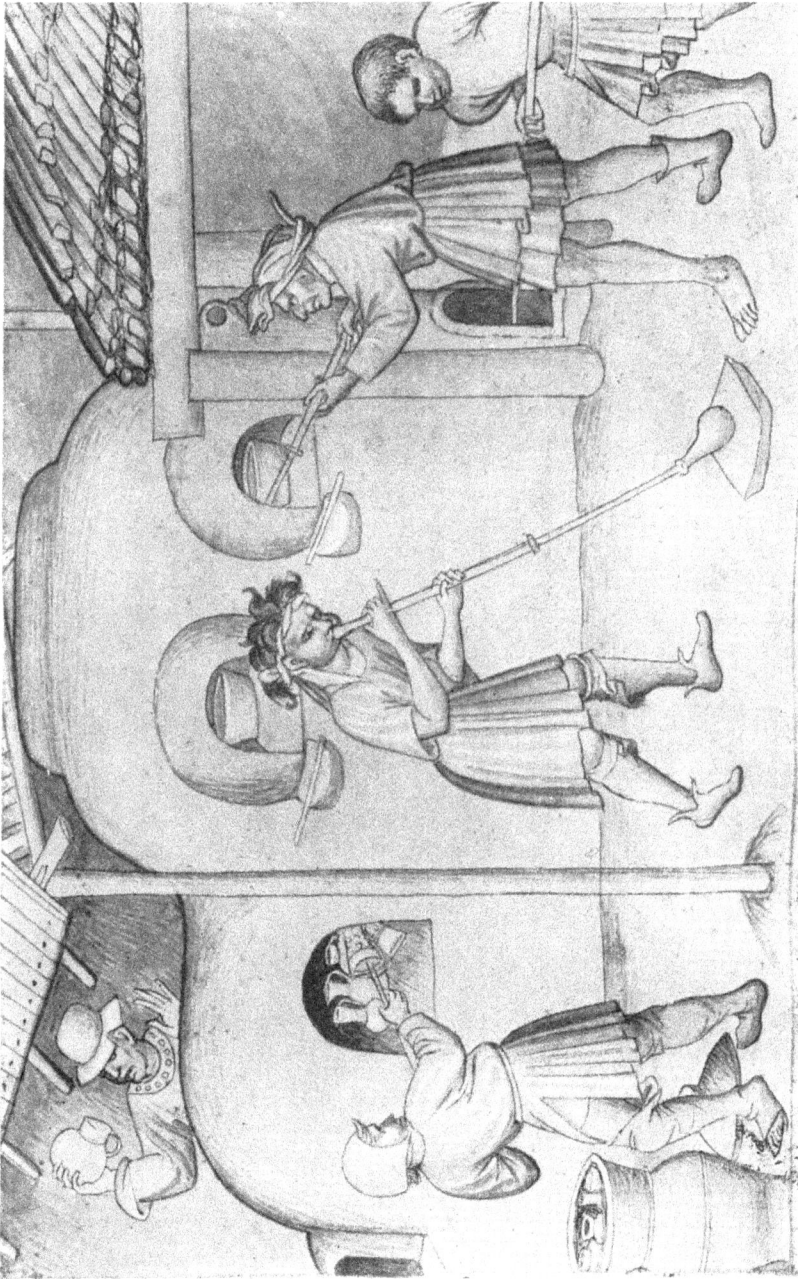

GLASS BLOWERS

The two outside figures show linen *under* shirts. The central figure is working in this under shirt only

[B.M. MS. Addl. 24189, 15c.]

AN ACTIVE GROUP OF MEDIÆVAL WOODWORKERS
Noah directing the building of the Ark.   Note differing head-dresses
[B.M. MS. Addl. 18850 (Bedford Hours), 15c.

APRON WEARERS

BOTH fishmongers on page 72 (B) and (F) wear the simple straight shirt-dress, made after the pattern No. 2 on page 73, so does the blacksmith. The last two have long fitted sleeves, but the fishmonger in the photo wears a shirt made exactly after the pattern on page 72 (F). It was made up in dark homespun tweed. An adaptation of this pattern is shown (page 73, No. 1) which may be found convenient, and may be used for almost any trade that does not require much leg work (shopkeepers, etc.), but the closed side seams should not be used for agricultural labourers or any active workers.

The apron, because it is so easy and effective, is a trap for the unwary costume-maker. *An* apron will not do, it must be *the* apron. What butler would deign to wear anything but green baize ? How the fringe on the grocer's apron would curl with horror to be tape-tied like a butcher's blue ! Your bench hand still slings his string over his head and your mechanic needs a boiler-suit. Mediæval people were just as particular. Fishmongers, butchers, shopkeepers in general wear aprons strapped in, pinned on, or tucked under, raised high or dropping low, but never stringed. The manual worker seems to favour strings (No. 2). Your doctor and surgeon have already fitted overalls (pages 19-21), but such an apron as page 73, No. 3, might be worn by an assistant or nurse attendant. The bag-apron (page 73, No. 4), which I found worn by a fat market woman, struck me as being very suitable for a children's nurse or comfortable old sewing-woman. The wearer of No. 5, page 73, has foresworn strings, and ties his apron behind his neck by the two top corners (the ends stick out like white rabbit's ears). Little work but much thought is required to give aprons their convincing quality. They are worth the trouble, in skilful hands, for they can be so characteristic. For men's wear, consider the job and get them begrimed in convincing places. Besides the bench dirt on the middle front, it is interesting to note that men, and working women, wipe their hands on their hips.

Also on a grubby apron there is usually a corner where they have wiped their fingers before taking it off, and an apron worn even twice has twisted strings.   The lady of the house wishful to appear very busy and domesticated makes a great flutter of white linen, and her poorer counterpart, who could not afford a new gown, has the satisfaction of a clean apron over the old one.

Curiously, the apron seems to be a badge of respectability that still holds in some districts.   The North countrywoman still wears a fine white apron, almost as part of her dress.   Over this a blue-checked one to keep it clean, over this a working-apron of strong holland, and sometimes she slips a coarse apron on top, before doing any dirty work. By the depth to which these layers are removed may be judged the status of the unexpected visitor.

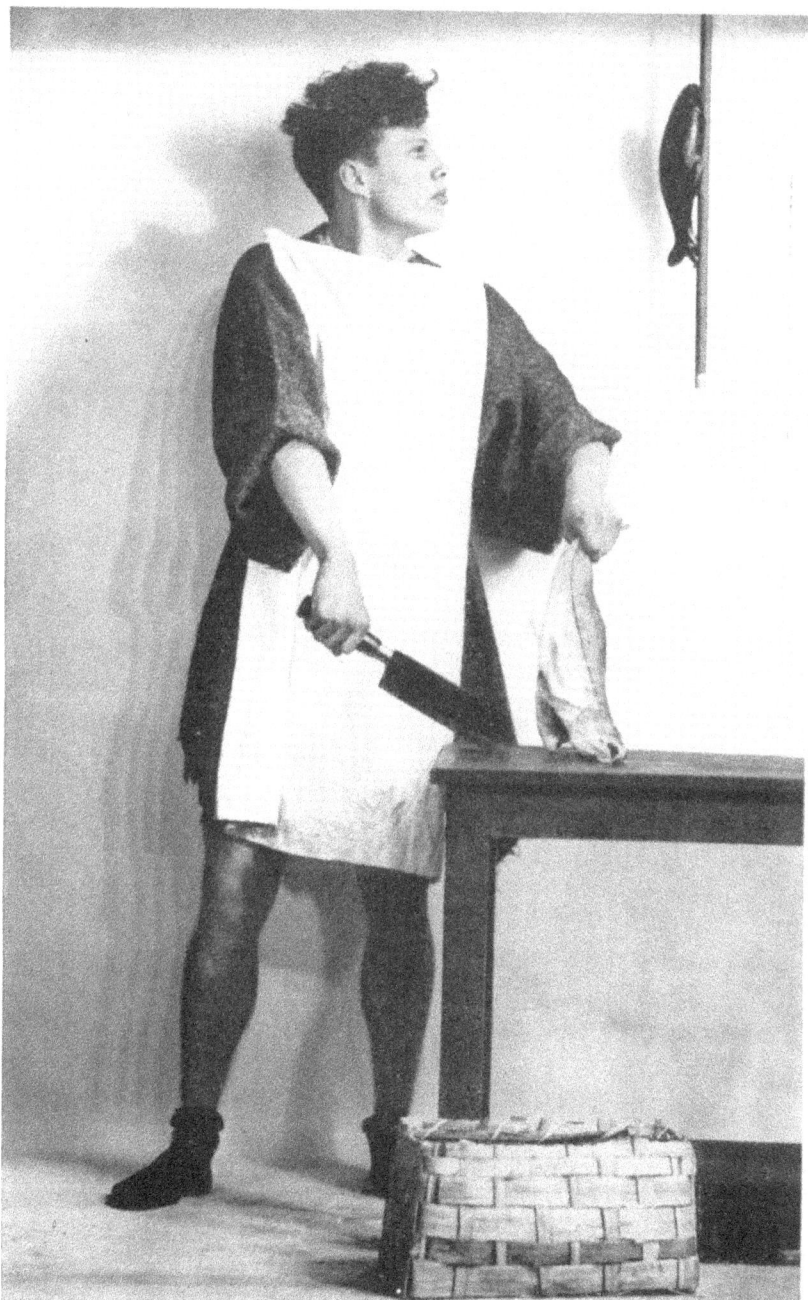

THE FISHMONGER, COMPLETE WITH APRON AND CHOPPER

MEDIÆVAL SALESFOLK AND HANDICRAFTSMEN, MALE AND FEMALE, WEARING DIFFERENT
TYPES OF APRON

(A)　[B.M. Facs. 198, 15c.]　　　　　(B)　[B.M. Facs. 18316, 14c.]
(C)　[Bodl. Liby. Ox. MS. 264, 14c.]　(D)　[B.M. MS. Harl. 6563, 14c.]
(E)　[B.M. MS. Kings, 9, 15c.]　　　　(F)　[Bodl. Liby. Ox. MS. Douce 6, 14c.]

SHOP·KEEPERS, AND ALL APRON·WEARERS

Plain foundation
shirt of any
suitable material
No·1

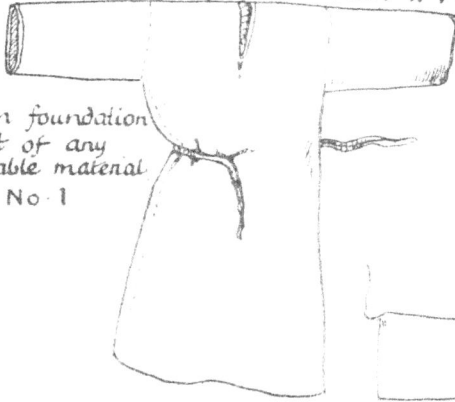

An Apron
with strings No·2

Corners tucked
under belt

High apron
for splashy
jobs.

No 3

Bag apron
market
woman or
nurse.
No·4.

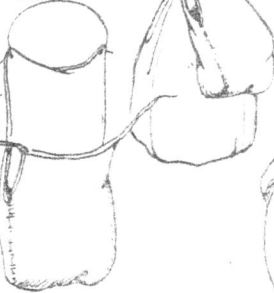

Corners of apron
tied round neck.
No·5.

For Leather
aprons.

AGRICULTURAL LABOURERS

REFER to pages 87-88 for the ploughman and herdsman. It is this type of labourer we are now clothing. The Irish and Welsh seem to have worn long trousers more than the dwellers in the south-east. A good example is shown on page 94 (B). The early mediæval people were very bad at making trousers. Most of the labourers who wear ' breeches ' appear to take a straight piece of stuff, pass it between their legs and tie it, by the front to the back corners, over each hip : it is in fact a mere breech clout. Others wore shorts : that is, they made two leg holes at the bottom of a wide bag (page 75, No. 2). These baggy discomforts were sometimes lashed up with strings (page 75, No. 3). In the large drawing (page 75) the shirt is swung upwards from the waist to show the probable reconstruction as given in the photograph on page 78. To make these ' breeches,' take an oblong piece of cloth rather more than a yard along its shorter edges, tie one of these shorter ends AA (page 75) around the waist, knotting it behind, and pull the other end backwards between the legs and knot it round in front. Now pull up the loose cloth, rolling the waist-line down over the knots till it makes a tight roll around the waist. A good close fit and comfortable wear can be attained by the skilful, and this twisted-up roll of cloth shows as a ridge through the outer dress just below the waist-line. Some of the figures in the MS. show this pattern very clearly.

The trousers (page 75, No. 4) may be used by shepherds and herds-men in general, but were not popular with quick-moving workers. They will be found comfortable, and look well if made ankle-length and cross-gartered upwards to the knee. Don't take the strapping above the knee, but finish it off with a few firm wrappings around the bony security where a navvy ties his trousers. The bottom part may be folded into the top of the boots or left to frill out over the bare feet. We have given a whole page to this subject of trousers because they are comfortable wear, but they are not at all characteristic mediæval clothing. In appearance every pair seems more impossible than the next (page 75, Nos. 2, 3, 4). But all mediæval trousers have one essential in making. They must be tied into the waist like pyjamas. This is absolutely essential, as it alters the movement of the wearer.

74

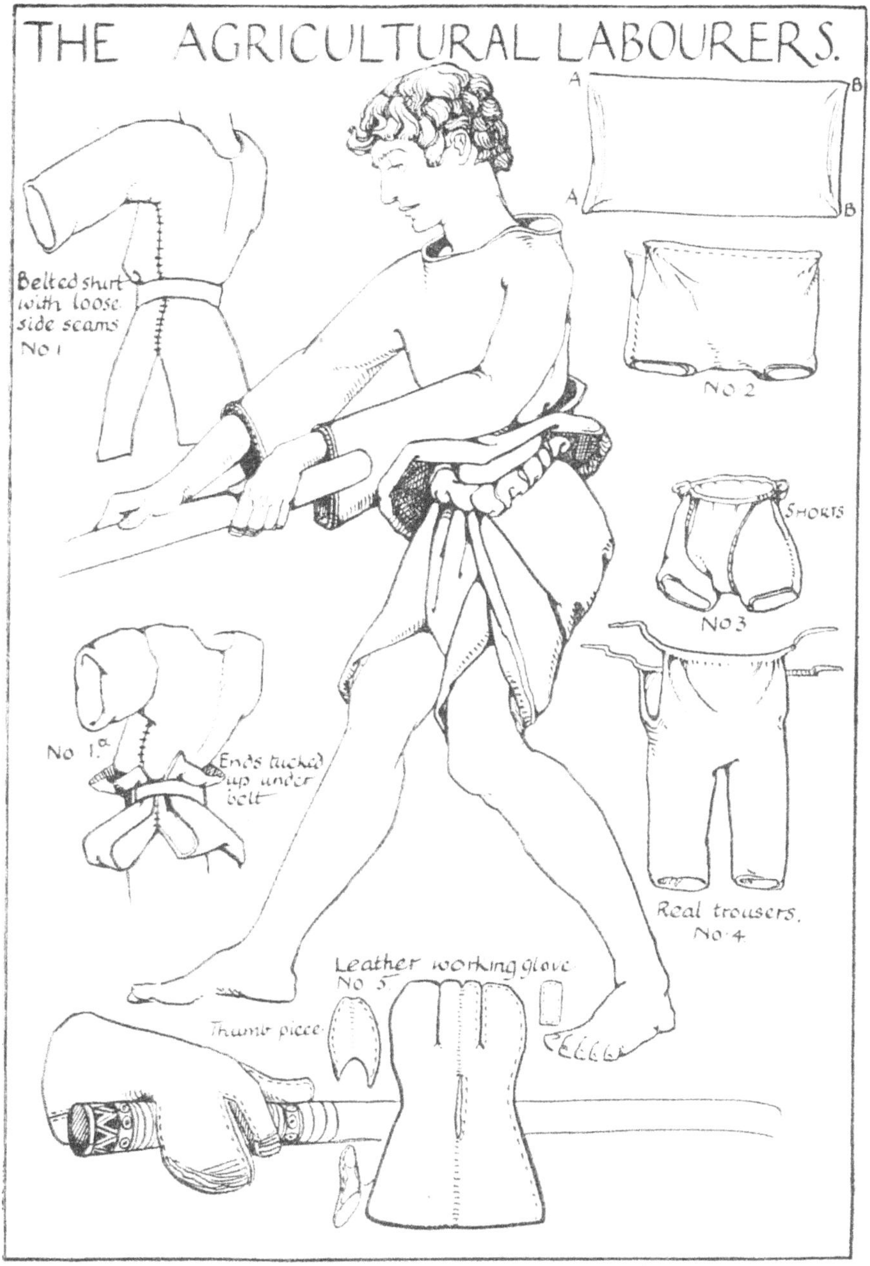
THE AGRICULTURAL LABOURERS.
A
B
A
B
Belted shirt with loose side seams No 1
No 2
Shorts
No 3
No 1.a
Ends tucked up under belt
Real trousers. No 4
Leather working glove No 5.
Thumb piece

String-hung trousers hang quite differently from those supported by adequate braces, and only string-hung trousers could hang badly enough to be mediævally convincing. The coat (page 75, No. 1) has two seams, one under each arm continuing down the sides. Leave the length below the waist open. In MS. (page 77) and the photo (page 78) this shirt is tucked up, and the sleeves rolled back.

The useful pattern on page 75 is worn as shown on the MS. on page 94, under their leather coats, and the flapping open of the side-pieces is very well shown. The coats on the figures, page 94, may be copied from page 73, No. 1, the hoods from page 93, and the shoes are drawn with other suitable leggings on page 83. The leather working-glove (page 75, No. 5) must be made by drawing around the wearer's hand, while he lays it flat down to make his own pattern. This should then be turned over to cut out the back of the same hand, but leave an appropriate space on the material before turning it over and repeating it, to allow for the thickness *through* the hand (page 75, No. 5). In the centre of this thickness, cut the slit into which the thumb is inserted (page 75, No. 5). The gusset pieces for the sides of the fingers (page 75, No. 5). The thumb tube should be cut to bring its seam outwards over the nail (page 75, No. 5), not on the inside, where it would come across the ball of the thumb. We have shown an ornamental whip-handle, but a simple and effective trick used by country boys, then and now, is to take dark-coloured sticks or willow wands and peel off the thin bark in fancy rings, which will give effective black and white stripes.

LABOURERS—ILLUSTRATIONS, FROM THE LUTTRELL PSALTER, 14 c.

Page 77.—(A). The figure sowing corn needs little or no explanation, but note whether it is to be a one-handed action or double-handed one, as the hopper is made differently.

(B). A word of description of this two-sticked weeding action. A weed-hook, a crotch and a glove were used for weeding; the crotch had a Y-shaped foot and with it you pressed down the head of the weed into the earth while you tweaked up the root with the hook, leaving the weed lying flat between the furrows. The crotch and hook and gloves are good properties.

(C). Feeding chickens: The woman's gown is good and the small light apron seems to be smocked into its band. The hen is tethered by the leg to a post in the ground—a useful point. The men's costume (D) is well shown and the flails are simple to construct.

(A)

(B)

(C)

(D)

A VARIETY OF FARMWORK FROM THE LUTTRELL PSALTER
Note the woman weeder's gloves
[All, B.M. MS. Luttrell Psalter, 14c.]

BACK VIEW OF A POOR LABOURER'S DRESS, WITH BREECH CLOUT, TAKING UP THE SACK

LABOURERS

THERE is now the poorer class of labourer, more difficult to describe, having no exact modern counterpart. You may need to include him in many cases, so before dressing him try to find out how he is attached to the rest of the community ; for cast-off clothes were handed down in mediæval days as they are to-day ; and the poorer worker in or near a town seems to be dressed differently from the poorer worker on the land. It is impossible to go into the mediæval intricacies of land-owner, freeman, bondman, etc. Agriculturists wear the most primitive of simple robes, but are very different in character to the workers. In most cases variations may be carried out in various materials, sometimes worn over breeches, often not. Where the belt is worn, the pleating round at the sides underneath it is noticeable. Where the sides are sewn up to the waist and worn without a belt, they are usually hitched up at the sides, giving the very characteristic crossfold drapery both in front and behind, seen so clearly on the MS. figures. It is certainly difficult to give the impression of poverty without dilapidation, or dilapidation without implying poverty, yet it is a mediæval attribute—we have not got the same thing now. For example, the most poverty-stricken worker all unwashed, with his single robe in rags and hair unkempt, may be wearing a most efficient and expensive-looking leather jerkin, because it was part of his work equipment. It may not have been his property at all, but the outward token of his master's claim upon his services, especially in connection with war or feudal field service, and so akin to ' livery.' Here we can, at best, only warn the costume-maker where to be careful and make inquiries. The labourer in the photograph (page 81) wears robe No. 1, on page 83, but without the belt. He has nothing underneath it, and this must be emphasised in wearing the costume—it is quite impossible to get the right effect over modern underclothing. The strap with which he carries the sack is one length only, and is likely to be leather rather than cord. Such a long strap may be slipped round almost any bulky

79

package in the loops, easy to do up and to loosen again.   The creel or back-basket (page 83, No. 2) is found in many forms in the MSS. ; some of them are practically the same as those in use to-day on the west coast of Ireland, in the islands off the coast of Scotland, or hill districts in the north of England.   If possible, get one of these.   Some of them have large, fan-shaped extensions rising high behind the head as No. 3, page 83 ; these are only used where the grass, dried peat, weed, bracken, brushwood, rushes, or other loads are very light but bulky.   They would be impossible to use piled high with turfs, earth or heavy material.   They are very arresting when the wearer walks about, as they sway up and down with the movement of the body.   If the creels cannot be obtained, simple forms may be made after this pattern.   Often a long pole (page 82 (D)) is inserted through the creel behind, long enough to reach to the ground and to form a rest for the wearer by grounding the weight of the basket when he leans back. The drawing MS. (page 82 (D)) puts this pole outside, but it will be seen how desperately uncomfortable such an arrangement would be. In use we have always found the pole inside the basket and the cross-pieces BB (page 83, No. 2) very well padded.   The bill-hook (page 83, No. 4) is found in many and varied forms and a modern version might be used.   The hat (page 83, No. 5) is a straw of plain shape.   Wet it and hang it on a pole to get this mediæval point.   The wheel-barrow, well illustrated in page 83, No. 6, is partly supported round the neck by a strap, though this is not an invariable rule.   The mediæval wheel-barrow appears more similar to the hand-barrow shown on page 82 (A) than the modern version—that is to say, the wheel is set in between the handles at the further end of the barrow more widely (leaving the same space between the sides in front as between the handles).   No. 6, page 83, shows this clearly.   The wheel-barrow is easily made and very effective.

   The leggings are illustrated on page 83.   They are often worn below the loose shirt.   Sometimes they are left loosely tied (page 83, No. 7), sometimes they are closely shaped to the limb (page 83, No. 8). Very often the lower ends of the awful mediæval trousers were bound up in this way and inserted into the boot-tops (page 83, No. 8A). Cloth hose and woollen socks are shown (page 83, No. 9).   The hose are made without feet, but with a loop under the instep (page 43, right-hand figure).   The socks are put over these, inside the boot.   A labourer coming indoors takes off his boots and walks in his stockinged feet, sits down by the fire, takes his socks off, hangs them up to dry, and spends the evening barefoot before the fire.   Sometimes the very long leg-wrap

THE LABOURER (page 78) CARRYING HIS SACK

(A)

(B)

(C)

(D)

(E)

LABOURERS ON LAND AND BUILDING AND BURDEN CARRIERS

(A) [Trin. C. Dublin MS. E. 1. 40, 13c.]   (B) [B.M. Facs. 190, 15c.]
(C) [B.M. MS. Addl. 38120, 14c.]   (D) [Bodl. Liby. Ox. MS. Douce 5, 14c.]
(E) [B.M. Facs. 227, 15c.]

LABOURERS.

Pattern of robe No. 1

Straw hat No. 5.

Bill hook No. 4

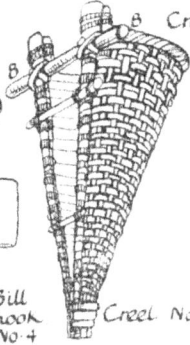

Creel. No. 2

B

B Creel carrier. No. 3

Wheel barrow No. 6

Wrapped Leggings. No. 7.

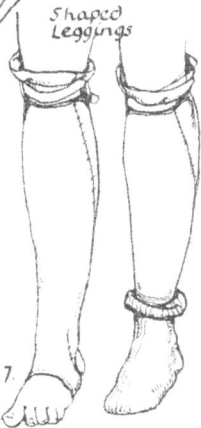

Leggings continued up the leg as hose...

Shaped Leggings

No. 8

A sock No. 9

Boots worn over leggings No. 8A

Padding the foot with the end of the wrapped legging No. 10

is continued down beyond the toes and then wrapped back under the foot and fastened behind up at the back of the heel as in page 83, No. 10. This makes comfortable soft walking. But realize that the cloth could not stand the wear of long-distance work and would look ridiculous on the feet of a walker, though it might serve to pad his shoes if they were large enough. Any of these simpler mediæval costumes depend upon the folds made by wear for their convincing quality. The more simple the dress, the longer and harder it should be worn to make it look convincing.

HINT.—Never fold these clothes in storing. The mediæval people are always represented as hanging them up by their necks or through their arm-holes and everybody who has had to deal with costumes realizes the effect this has upon them.

HERDSMEN

WE keep these distinct from agricultural workers, but study the possible interchange of some of the clothes. The MS. on page 87, from which photo (A) on page 87 is taken, shows trousers (cf. page 94 (B)), and a long smock made after pattern on page 83, but longer, and with the front and back width plainly overlapped (not gathered). The hood is simple, and may be made after patterns on page 93. In the MS. figure (page 87 (B)), the shepherd wears a straw or felt hat over his cloth hood. Such hats may have been purposely made with these high, pointed crowns; though others, of less 'worn' aspect, appear flat. The easiest way to achieve the pointed effect is to hang an ordinary straw hat up, wet and heavy, on a pole for some time. By wetting and replacing it repeatedly to hang on the pole you can achieve the shape exactly, but whether it was intentional or not is a mediæval mystery. The hood is made on the same principle as the inturned sack, worn by a modern coal-carter to prevent scrubbing his neck with a heavy sack. This head-dress was worn exactly the same way, for the same reason, by mediæval sack-carriers, and is simple and effective, but note that mediæval sacks seem slightly shorter than ours. To make the hood, take a squarish sack (page 93, No. 1), fold one corner B into corner A (page 93, No. 2), slip it on to the head, and mark just below the point of the jaw-bone, through both thicknesses of the sack. Cut through the inner part of the hood and pull forward the bottom part over the shoulders at this line, leaving a double head part and a wide neck-wrap (page 93, No. 3). Put the hood on, and complete the fitting as shown (page 93, Nos. 4 and 5). For a slender, tight fit around the neck, note that the double thickness of the top part leaves off just below the ears, and the darts are made through the single material around the neck. Run the darts upwards towards the ear and towards the centre back of the head (page 93, No. 5). The shoulder may be cut up once, or twice, to give a smooth fit to the yoke part front and back. If liked, the square unwanted ends of the neck-wrap (that fold over beyond the centre fastenings) may be halved into two triangles, and inserted as four triangular gussets around the shoulder line. This is a good well-

fitting hood, very comfortable in wear.   Below (page 93, No. 6) is a
hood cut squarely with a centre slit for the face, leaving the two points
on either side of the head.   These points well stuffed and tied up can
begin the donkey's ears of a fool's cap and be developed into the jester's
head-dress.

The long liripipe hood may be achieved in either of two ways
(page 93, Nos. 7 and 8).   The easiest way to make this pipe (or any
such long tube) is a simple trick.   Sew it up on the outside, drop a
bodkin down inside, catch that bodkin by a stitch or two through the
material at the bottom and thread it backwards—up and inside out
(page 93, No. 8).   The plain hood (page 93, No. 10) is a common and
popular form.   The face shows in the opening in the front and the point
drops behind the head, and the wide part concertinas down over the neck
and shoulders.   Laid flat, it is of course a plain triangle folded into a
cone and a true mediæval pattern, as will be seen (page 93, No. 8), but it
is apt to look bulky if not well adjusted, especially upon small figures.

HINT.—If the face-opening slips about, it can usually be steadied
by a band of stitching passing over the top of the head from ear to ear,
fastening down the *underside* of the point into a flap.   We do not
recommend this hood for comfort or appearance, but it may be very
useful where a hood must be slipped on or off swiftly.   The boots
(page 93, No. 11) are of soft leather, worn over woollen socks and
bound around the ankles with their own ties.   Sometimes these ties
are a strand of leather rolled cordwise and sufficiently long to criss-
cross down the boot, and, we believe, were sometimes tied round
under the instep.   The bagpipes (page 93, No. 12) are an early form,
one skin bag and two pipes.   We can give you the appearance of the
instrument, but you must consult a musician about the noise it made.
A man on page 87 (D) wears a gown, bare legs and leather shoes with
crossed ties.   For his hood (page 57, No. 2) and horn (page 57, No. 4).

Every shepherd or herdsman will have a tarbox, a bag to take his
food with him to the grazing grounds, and a pipe of some sort for
music.   A leather bottle would carry his drink for the day, and he
would probably take a cloak.   Many shepherds (on page 88) would
have 'their dog unto their girdle tied' and the dog might wear a
spiked collar (page 93, No. 13).   Swineherds (page 87 (C)) would take
long cudgels in the autumn to whack down the acorns, and a goose-
herd or neatherd would have a long rod-pole or perch.

Note the gaiter-like canvas leggings tied under the knee, on pages
87 (C) and 88 (B); both these herdsmen carry netted bread-bags
(hence Fr. *panier*) at their girdles, resembling miniature hammocks.

(A)

(B)

(C)

(D)

(A) THE SHEPHERD

(B) THE ORIGINAL PICTURE [B.M. MS. Egerton, 1894, 14c.]

(C) A CARVED CLOAKED SWINEHERD [Statue, Cluny Museum, Paris]

(D) PLOUGHING WITH A PAIR OF OXEN [B.M. Facs. 59 C.R. 7. E. 15c.]

(B)

(A)

(D)

(C)

Field and Farm Workers in various Attitudes with Cloaks and Hoods.　(B) Modern-looking Gaiters

(A) [B.M. MS. Addl. 17280, 15c.]　(B) [Bodl. Liby. Ox. MS. 15c.]　(C) & (D) [B.M. MS. Luttrell Psalter, 14c.]

CONCERNING HOODS

THE hood may, in principle at least, be accounted a part of primæval clothing. The Greeks and Romans for the most part normally walked abroad with heads uncovered. When, for one reason or another, it became desirable to be 'covered,' this was usually done by drawing the cloak up to act as a veil. The next step would naturally be to pin or otherwise fasten the front edge of the drapery together at the throat. From this to a hooded cloak of the burnoose kind the transition appears obvious. It seems worth while to dwell in some detail on the evolution of the hood and its offshoots, since they are so characteristic a feature of mediæval apparel from the Crusades to the Wars of the Roses. It seems probable that the ultimate ancestor of the mediæval hood was the Roman *paenula*, a species of cloak akin to a 'poncho,' among whose other derivatives are the liturgical chasuble and cope. This was worn for travelling and rough weather, and from its obvious convenience came to be worn to some extent even by the better classes, in proportion as the lordly toga ceased to be *the* prescriptive full-dress habit of a Roman citizen. It was closed (wholly or in part) by a single seam down the front (so that it had to be drawn over the head), reached well below the knees, and was mostly fitted with a pointed cowl. Closed as it was all round, its length was early found to hamper the motions of the arms unduly, and hence was very soon modified in a variety of ways. The hood began fairly early in the Middle Ages to be adapted to a variety of cloaks and upper-garments. As an independent garment protecting only head, neck and shoulders it does not seem to have come into vogue until the twelfth century was some three-quarters spent. Thenceforward it rapidly becomes perhaps the most typical headgear of the Middle Ages. It is worn alone or in conjunction with other kinds of head-dresses : for very soon we find diverse hats and caps worn over the hood, a fashion that recurs frequently to the close of the Middle Ages. The converse (that is the wearing of caps, etc. *under* the hood) also occurs ; though not common, except in the case of the close *coif* of linen that, first appearing at the close of the twelfth century, survived, as part of the lawyer's robes, as late as

Elizabethan days. In order to understand what the *coif* was the reader should refer to the section ' Medical and Scientific ' (pages 18-22). The hoods of the Middle Ages display considerable variety, and no mean degree of ingenuity is shown in some of the patterns. Those particularized in the section on ' Herdsmen ' (pages 85-88 and 93-94) by no means exhaust the possibilities. There were hoods made in two uniform halves and others cleverly contrived out of a single piece of material ; the liripipe or long tail at the back being either cut in one with the headpiece or separately fashioned and sewn on.[1] Not the least clever piece of contrivance is the manner in which some of these liripipes are fitted to the hoods. These tail-like extensions of the peak of the hood are hardly in evidence, by the way, till after 1300. About the same date a new fashion of wearing the hood begins to appear. Indeed the variety of ways in which this type of head-dress could be worn no doubt largely accounts for its long-drawn vogue. It could be (*a*) drawn over the head so as to cover the head, neck and shoulder, or (*b*) the cowl could be thrown back on the shoulders, so that it merely formed a warm shoulder-wrap, or (*c*) in warm weather it could be doffed at a moment's notice and simply slung over one shoulder like a scarf. Now comes in a fourth way of adapting it for wear : it formed a kind of turban-cap, the head being inserted through the face-opening. The liripipe and cape then hung down fore and aft or on either side. This, it has been suggested, was a foppish invention : it seems originally to have been the natural outcome of the tendency to cover the head without muffling up the neck and shoulders. The long liripipe was already beginning to be wound round the body of the hood, confining it at the temples. With the new turban-like disposal of the hood, the cape and liripipe were increasingly twisted together and arranged in a great variety of forms.

This applies particularly to ' dressy ' folk, and is very notable about the close of the fourteenth and early fifteenth centuries, when much versatility was shown in differentiating the hoods. Towards 1420 these elaborated arrangements are largely superseded by a new ' made up ' variant commonly referred to by antiquaries as a *chaperon*,[2] by

---

[1] A most interesting series of actual hoods, to say nothing of caps, hose and tunics for both sexes--dating from the fourteenth century and earlier—were unearthed in southern Greenland in 1921. See Dr. Poul Norlund : ' Buried Norsemen at Herjolfsnes ' in *Meddelser om Grønland*, vol. lxii ; Copenhagen, 1924.

[2] The word is merely the generic French term for a hood, though it is also extended to include this specific form, which has lost all the distinctive features of the primeval hood.

which term we also shall for convenience' sake denote it. Possibly something of the sort existed from about 1400 or even earlier, but it is not till about 1420 that we can confidently identify it. The elaborately twisted and draped turban-hood needed time and taste to arrange in becoming folds, and was over-apt to become disordered on slight provocation. Hence no doubt the popularity of the chaperon, as being at once picturesque and convenient; at any rate it remained *the* characteristic wear of the better classes till *c.* 1460, though worn much later by professional men and in the robes of certain knightly orders. The basis of the chaperon was a wreath-like pad, called a *bourlet* or *roundlet* (not unlike a miniature motor-tyre), encircling the temples. To the inner rim of this were transferred and adapted the liripipe and shoulder-cape of the old hood; the latter gathered into folds and draped *ad lib.* over the roundlet like a loose skirt, the former trailing on one side like a long scarf, which could be wound round the neck, thrown over the opposite shoulder or passed through the belt. With few exceptions the whole of this erection was uniform in fabric and colour, though the lining of the skirt, when visible, may differ. Liripipe and skirt could be as variously arranged as could the hood whence they derived, without any of its attendant inconveniences, and could be so disposed as to subserve most of its objects. Incidentally it is not at all uncommon to find the chaperon worn over a close hood of the older fashion. The hood proper was commonly so cut that the facial opening projected far beyond the face. As normally worn, this front edge was commonly turned back or rolled outward to frame the face more closely. It was this reversed or rolled edge, generally found with hoods worn turban-wise, that doubtless suggested the roundlet of the chaperon. The latter is sometimes made without a liripipe, naturally never without the gathered 'skirt.' On the other hand, when the hood and chaperon ceased to be fashionable, the liripipe, in the form of a long scarf, was often adapted to the brim of the modish hats, to serve the same purpose it had regularly fulfilled when the chaperon was momentarily doffed : *i.e.* it hung down in front as a counterweight to the head-dress slung behind the shoulder. We may as well add here that the edges of the hood were from a fairly early date[1] cut into 'dagges'—*i.e.* a border resembling a row of petals or leaves—first the shoulder-cape, then the facial opening, ultimately the later form of liripipe. These 'daggings' were at times separate pieces sewn on. They first become conspicuous in fourteenth-century

---

[1] There seems to be evidence of something of the sort as early as the twelfth century.

costume, but their heyday was from *c.* 1385-1440. From about the middle of the fourteenth century to the early part of the fifteenth the hoods not infrequently fitted closely into the neck, being close-buttoned in front from chin to breast.

The shoulder-cape or *pélerine* as an independent garment appears to have come in about the middle of the fourteenth century. In many cases, however, what resembles a cape is probably intended for a hood with the cowl thrown back, and the former would scarcely seem to have enjoyed very extensive patronage.

A few words finally may not be out of place concerning the feminine versions of the hood. What distinguishes these (as opposed to the earlier veils, wimples, etc. that covered the ladies' heads of an earlier age) from their male counterparts is that the edges, instead of being sewn or buttoned, hang free, leaving chin and throat exposed (they could be separately covered by a wimple or gorget). The liri-pipe followed the same development as in the men's hoods. Other-wise the dimensions, cut and arrangement of the loose ' skirts ' were largely a question of individual taste ; but the gradual evolution of this type into the sixteenth-century ' kennel ' and ' French hood ' and their derivatives can be continuously traced.

F. M. K.

HERDSMEN AND HOODS

No. 1

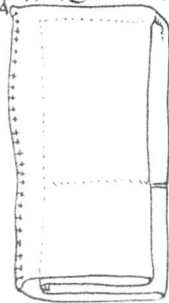

No. 2

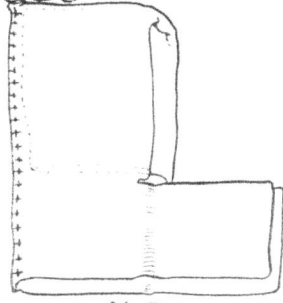

No. 3

The fitting of the hood. No. 4 & 5

Shoulder and neck-pieces

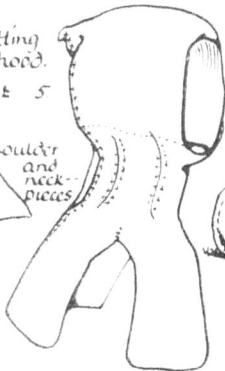

Dog and leather bottle No. 13

The two pointed hood. No. 6

No. 9

Bodkin

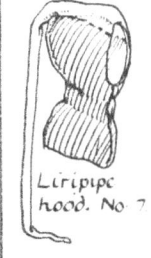

Liripipe hood. No. 7

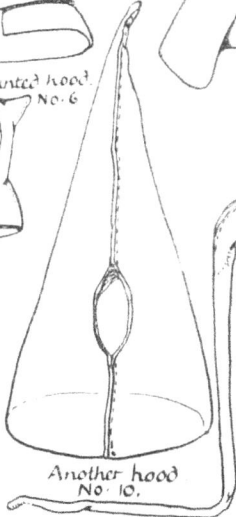

Another hood No. 10.

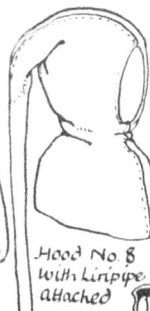

Hood No. 8 with Liripipe attached

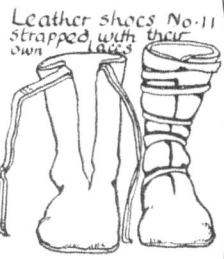

Leather shoes No. 11 strapped with their own laces

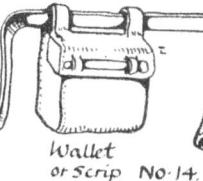

Wallet or Scrip No. 14.

Bag Pipe No. 12

(A)　　　　　　　　　　　　　　(B)

(C)

(D)

(E)

COUNTRY WORKERS' COSTUMES, CHIEFLY OF SAXON DATE, WITH THE SHORT TROUSERS,
TUNIC AND BARE LEGS

(A)　[13th century. Bible Moralisée. B.M. Facs. 169, 13c.]
(B)　[12th century. B.M. Cott. MS. Nero C. IV.]
(C) to (E)　[B.M. MS. Harl. 603, 11c.]

NOTE

Apart from casual illustrations, such as have for the most part been drawn upon here, there are certain well-defined groups of miniatures in mediæval MS. which may be confidently turned to for information as to the manifold operations of the countryside, and the appearance, implements and methods of their practitioners. Foremost come the calendar illuminations appended to the psalters and Horae. These portray for us, in great abundance and variety, all the occupations appropriate to the different seasons of the year. From their incessant recurrence we may learn how intimately dependent upon the land and its fruits was the whole scheme of mediæval life. Even the townsman of the Middle Ages grew up with the country, so to speak, at his very door, and could never for long be unaware of it.

The other group of subjects is culled from the Bible. In the Old Testament agricultural and pastoral scenes are frequent ; in the New Testament the favourite subject is the Annunciation to the shepherds.

Both groups of subjects formed favourite motives in the sculptured church-fronts and painted windows. In literature the *locus classicus* is doubtless Jean de Brie's *Le bon Berger*, written about 1379 : a work almost photographic in its detailed description of a mediæval shepherd.

F. M. K.

THE FULL SKIRT

MEDIÆVAL people went to extremes—a full circular skirt measured about 15 yards around the hem. This is achieved very simply when you know how to do it. There are no complicated gores nor shaped pieces in the pattern—it is evolved direct from straight lengths of material—and the fitting is done on the figure after the lengths have been joined up (as shown on the right side of the diagram, p. 99).

The amount of material depends upon the height of the wearer from neck to foot.

In diagram (page 99), supposing the dress to be $1\frac{1}{2}$ yards from neck to hem (an average 5 ft. 6 ins. figure), a 3-yard piece is laid down in two $1\frac{1}{2}$-yard lengths to form front and back of the gown. For reasons that will presently be apparent, the fold comes at the *bottom* of the gown.

A measurement is then taken from shoulder to waist-line at the side, and—supposing this to be $\frac{1}{2}$ yard—then eight extra widths of material are added on either side of the skirt, each piece being 2 yards long, and the fold again coming at the hem end.

This gives us a central body (back and front) piece one width wide, and an extended skirt piece five widths wide (front and back). See diagram, page 99.

Join up all selvedges YY on each side and also the level side seam SS. These extra side widths, cut level sideways and then left to open and fall downwards from waist to hem, are the essence of the whole pattern.

There is now a sleeveless princess body piece with a wide extension at either side forming the skirt.

The whole dress should now be laid flat down upon the floor, when it will appear as No. 1 on page 99. Now take the measurement S-X and mark off the hem of the circular skirt X-S. (The additional side widths should have enlarged the skirt so far on either side as to permit of the measurements SX and SS being equal, which is not actually the case here.)

This being done on both sides, the completely circular hem of the skirt is turned up, the top of the side seam strengthened by a small pleat where it runs up into the side seam of the bodice, and the full skirt is finished.

It will measure from 12 to 15 yards around the hem without *any* fullness around the waist or any additional gores or pleatings to the skirt : a marvel of mediæval constructive genius ! But there is greater ingenuity to follow !

The sleeves are made from the two triangular pieces left over after the semicircle of the skirt has been cut out. Mediæval forethought, by placing the fold of the material at the *hem* end of the skirt pieces, thus avoided a seam along the top of the sleeve. This piece (sleeve piece) is shown at the top right-hand corner of page 99.

To set-in this sleeve, hold out the arm level with the shoulder and lay the folded bottom edge X-X-X along the top of the arm H-X. One point of the triangle will curve up against the neck, the opposite point will hang down to E, and the curved side of the triangle will come under the arm A-E.

Mark the shoulder and cut off the neck point, A ; open this piece out and insert it as a gusset under the arm-hole. (A glance at the diagrams A-A will show this clearly.)

This piece is set backwards and down into the underarm seam, and let-in between the front and back of the bodice pieces. It will probably need easing under the arm and the chief fitting is done here.

We have found it simplest to make up the sleeve as shown (complete sleeve) and slip it on over a fitted bodice to which it can be tacked into place ; the robe is then slipped on over the sleeve (with its side seams left open and shoulder seams pinned and the bodice fitted down over the sleeve pieces), but this point may be left to the dressmaker's discretion : for this part is far more simply done than explained upon paper.

The pointed end E is then cut off and laid backwards along the lower end of the sleeve seam to form the characteristic round end E.

Note.—Whether this point is cut off higher or lower depends upon the designer's own ideas. If cut off much higher up (for example where the old skirt join Y *crosses* the sleeve material) then the sleeve becomes almost square, and gives (with a judicious ' pleat ' at the join) the effect of huge square cuffs.

The dress is now ready for its final fitting to the figure. Small pleats may be taken in at the waist-line, back and front, and if a back fastening is arranged for, fitting may be made very close. Shoulder seams should be sloped as much as possible, as the under-arm gusset permits of a comfortable fit.

In fact, any individual fitting that may be done to mould the bodice closely to the figure is permitted. The remnants of clothes and dresses actually copied from the originals show as many and varied seams as there are gowns. But all go to prove that they are the result of fittings done *on the figure*—not previously cut in the material.

Edges may be adorned as desired. Fur was popular, also faced hems of contrasting material. If a belt is worn, see that it is at least 3 inches wide and fits well above the side points S-S. Any fullness in the bodice should be discreetly pleated away and any fullness below the belt discreetly encouraged.

The infinite variety of the dresses that are based upon this fundamentally simple design is a mediæval marvel. If two or more dresses are cut out at the same time the exchange of sleeve pieces or interchange of points A and E may be tried.

Extra lengths may be added to the sleeves to form long knotted-ended hangings.

Making one or more of the side widths of a different material gives an interesting diagonal colouring across the skirt.

The neck opening may be extended to the edge of the shoulders, and furthermore widened by breadths of velvet, fur, or even fine gauze. Occasionally the sleeves were made tight-fitting to the wrist, when the ' spare ' material would be made into ' flappers ' to fall down over the hands—or even made into curious little capelike frills behind the shoulders. It was an excellent shape to show off the pattern of a rich brocade ; a useful shape for thick woollen cloth for a stately matron, and in lighter materials made beautiful folded drapery around the feet of a dancing maiden without overweighting her slender waist.

To Wear.—Call upon your gods ; put your weight upon your heels and practise. Remember when going up steps to raise the knee high and spread the folds forward with a skilful movement of the foot beneath the skirt to avoid treading upon the hem. Dancing with a blanket pinned to each shoulder, and hanging down in front of you, is practice not to be despised, and before stepping backwards make a half-turn sideways, so that the folds subside gracefully forwards. You can then pass away out amidst your flowing drapery like a retreating tide. Also learn to pick up the hem of your skirt (at the exact point S

THE VERY FULL CIRCULAR SKIRT.

No 1
One width of material forms back and fronts of gown. Two more widths are added each side to form the wide skirt

End piece cut off for gusset under arm.

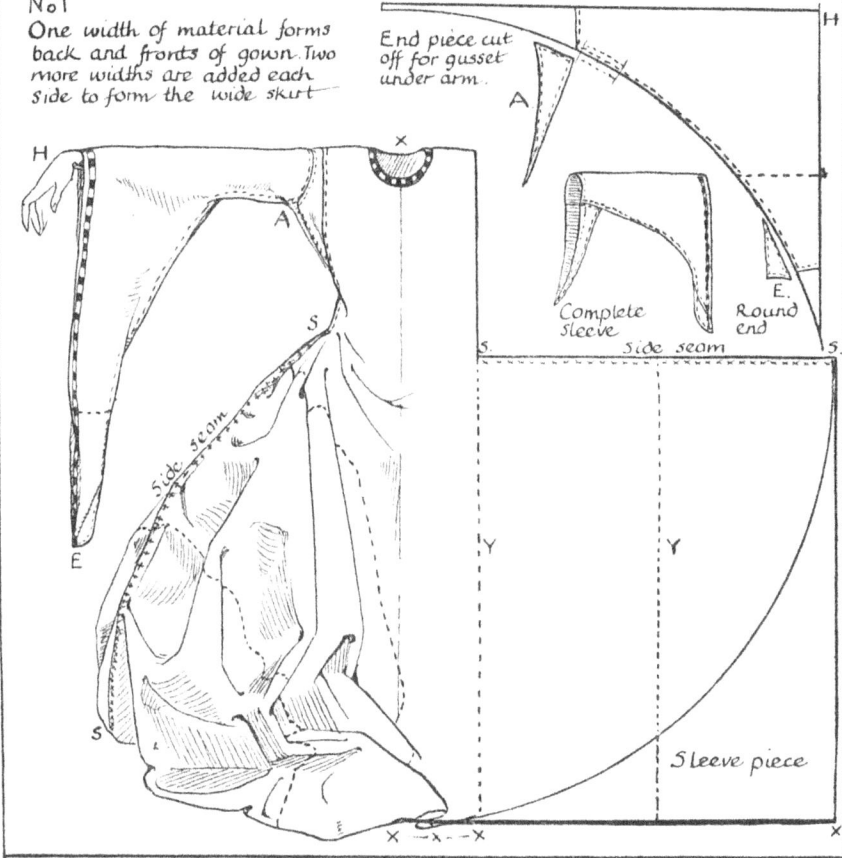

A

H

×

H

A

S

Complete Sleeve

E.
Round end

S   Side seam   S

Side seam

E

Y   Y

S

Sleeve piece

× — × — ×   ×

at the lower end of the side seam), and sweeping the whole side extension up and over your arm to form a complete circle for a statuesque
moment. The mediæval wearers were *very* expert at this—but no
author would attempt to describe to any woman, mediæval or modern,
the infinite variety of the very full circular skirt.

A COURT SCENE WITH A LONG TRAIN AND BEARER ; A STUDY IN VARYING HEAD-DRESSES

Note the high official's fur-trimmed coat and chain of office

[B.M. Facs., *Histoire de Helayne*, 15c.]

Ladies' Dresses

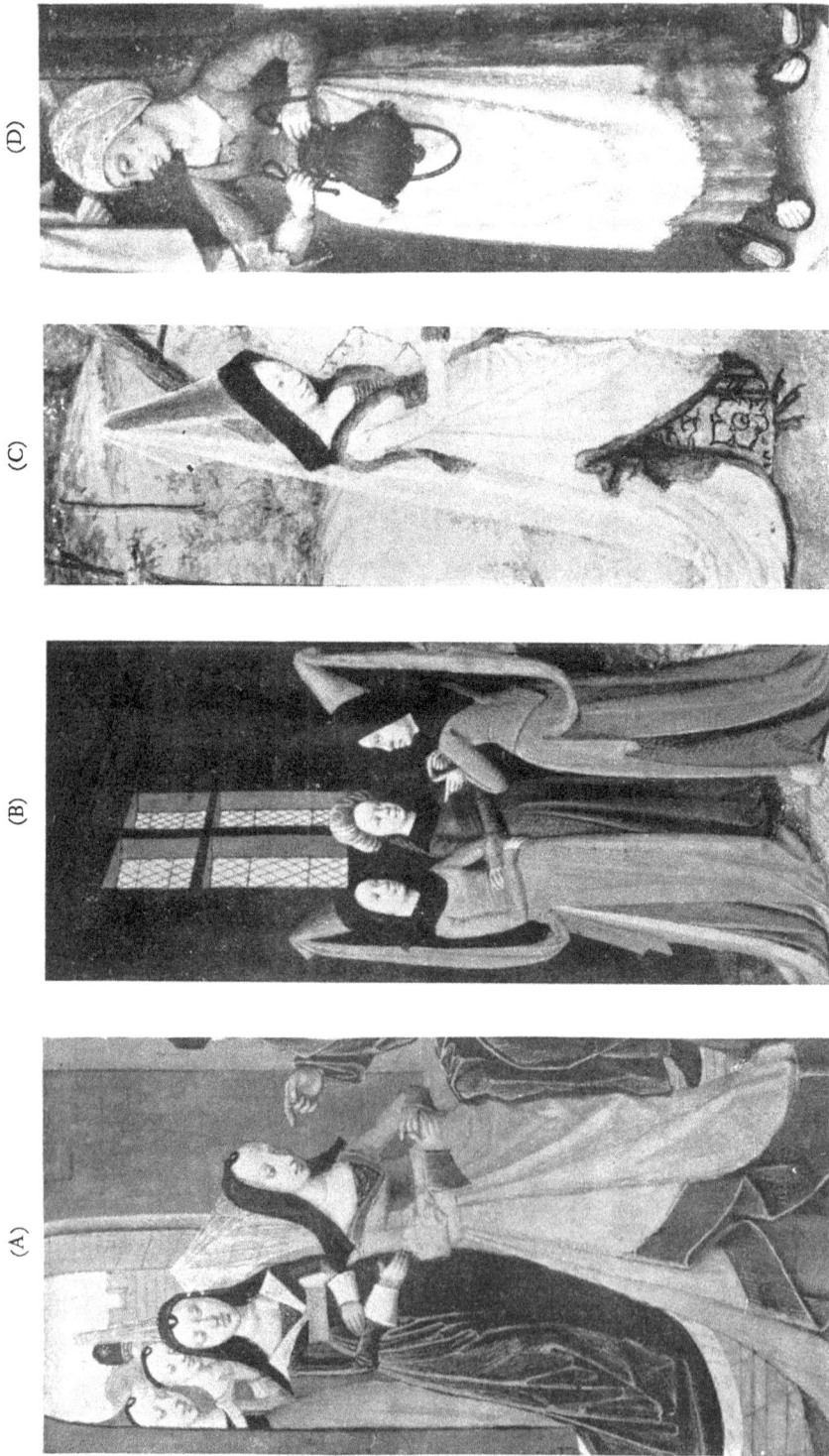

A COMPARATIVE VIEW OF FIFTEENTH-CENTURY HEAD-DRESSES AND SKIRTS, WITH AN EXCELLENT BAG

(A) [B.M. Roy. MS. 18. E. IV. late 15c.]   (B) [B.M. MS. Harl. 4375, 15c.]   (C) [B.M. Roy. MS. 15. D. III. 15c.]   (D) [B.M. MS. Harl. 4425, 15c.]

LADIES "DRESSES"

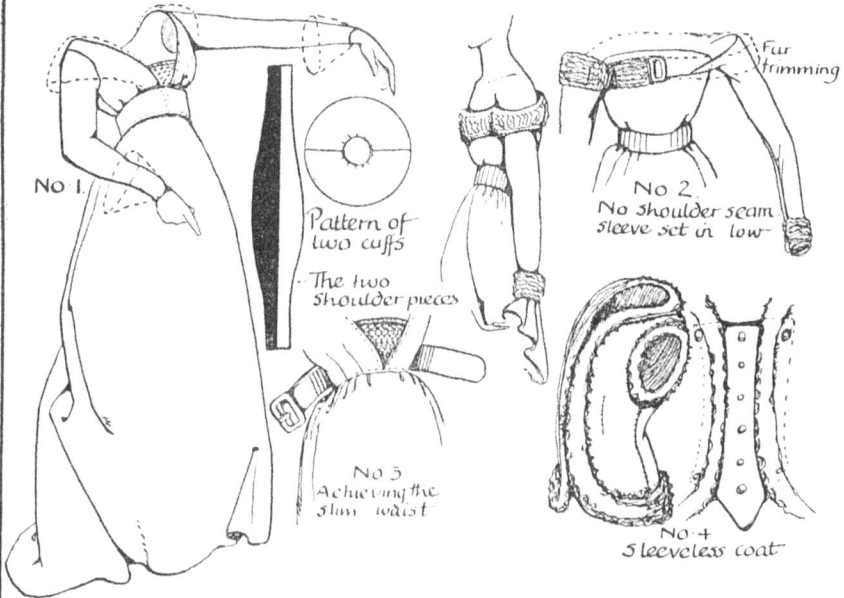

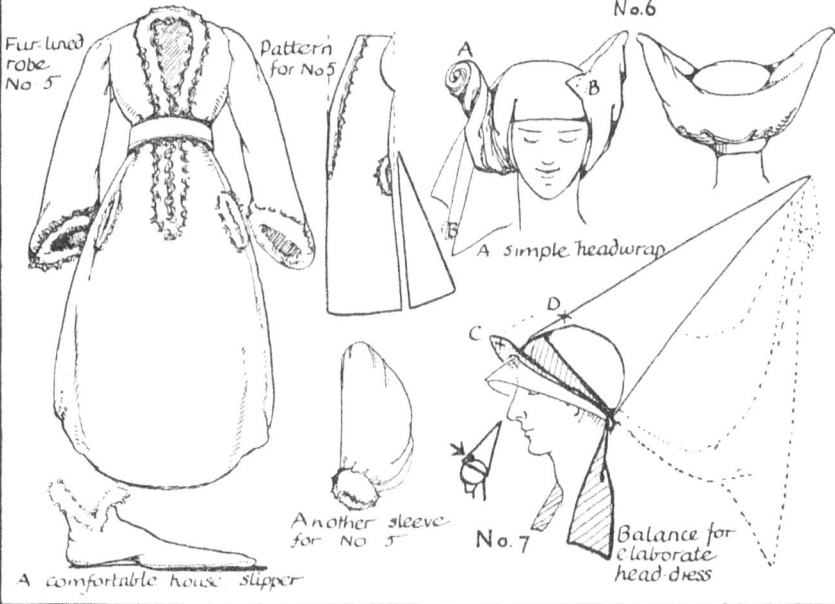

No 1

Pattern of two cuffs

The two shoulder pieces

No 3
Achieving the slim waist

Fur trimming

No 2
No shoulder seam sleeve set in low

No 4
Sleeveless coat

Fur-lined robe
No 5

Pattern for No 5

No.6

A simple headwrap

Another sleeve for No 5

A comfortable house slipper

No. 7

Balance for elaborate head-dress

LADIES' DRESSES

ONCE the full circular skirt has been constructed and studied, the following dresses need little explanation other than the photos and diagrams offered.

No. 1, page 103, explains the elaborate dresses on page 102. The neck is slit down to the waist in front and cut low around the shoulders. The robe may also be cut as in No. 3, where the full skirt is gathered on to the bodice. In these waisted fittings be sure the belt comes exactly above (*not over*) the waist seam to achieve the slim waist effect and fullness of the skirt below the tight bodice. There is a small triangular vest which prevents the open bodice entirely parting company and slipping down off the shoulders in two halves. This perilous possibility is emphasised by the two epaulettes or very low wide shoulder pieces added upon either side. These stand out over the sleeve tops and do much to make the neck and waist above and below appear abnormally slender. The flaring circular cuffs achieve the same effect for the wrist.

No. 2, page 103, is the inevitable end of pattern No. 1, page 103. No. 4, page 103, shows a sleeveless jacket which must have been comforting in draughty halls—it may be fur-lined or only fur-trimmed—and the curious let-in front panel may be variously trimmed but is definitely part of the jacket. This front seems to have been stiffened by light strips of wood or whalebone and the jacket secured to it firmly by metal studs or clasps. The whole jacket is essentially a sturdy little affair, and though in some cases it seems to have been worn as part of the robe, we believe it was always made and put on separately. Do not confuse it with the gowns which have large side-pieces of a different material let in at the side under the arms. Though these large side-pieces might be outlined with fur, and give the appearance of a jacket, they did not give the same effect in wear.

No. 5, page 103, is a fur-lined robe that would comfort *any* elderly mediæval matron. Made of good thick brightly-coloured dark cloth,

(A)

(B)

(C)

(D)

LATE GOTHIC LADIES' COSTUMES WITH ACCESSORIES LIKE BELTS, BEADS AND BAGS

(A) THE VISITATION [B.M. MS. Addl. 38126, 15c.]

(B) WEEPER ON BEAUCHAMP TOMB, St. Mary's, Warwick, 15c.]

(C) [Figure from a Tomb in the Cluny Museum, 15c.]

(D) [B.M. MS. Harl. 4425, 15c.]

FOUR DIGNIFIED MEDIÆVAL FLEMISH LADIES Flemish, first half of 15c. Casts in V. & A. Museum]

[Brass statuettes by Jacques de Gerines, Rijks Museum, Amsterdam.

lined with black or brown fur, and a broad gold and black belt, it would be dignified and handsome, and the muff-like pocket-holes, widely set up on either side, give a lovely bulgy look—a warmly opulent gown. If fur-lining throughout is impracticable, line with thick blanketing and fur the openings extra deeply, but see the belt be broad and strong. Below is a comfortable house slipper that might well be made of the same leather as the belt.

A SIMPLE HEAD-WRAP (page 103, No. 6).—A simple horned effect may be made by a skilful adjustment of the ordinary head-wrap. And *note* that when horns are fashionable the simple folk are apt to twist their head-wrap hornways, and when high divided head-dresses are worn by the grand ladies then the stiff linen head-wraps of the village ladies are folded and pleated into a similar outline. To achieve this effect for a mediæval woman with her simple head-wrap, take a fairly large square piece of rather stiff thick linen and bind the middle of one side around the forehead, securing it behind the head over the rest of the cloth. Let the two shortened corners hang down towards the front ; the two longer corners (at the opposite side of the square from the forehead side) will hang down the back (as B on the left). Take the front short corners and twist them up into circular pointed cones high above the ears (as shown at A) ; secure these and shape them cunningly as desired. Then lift up the back piece B-B with a rolling motion and bring the corners around to the front, enclosing the ears and wrapping up the ' horns ' you have made (as at B, right side). The back view shows the completed effect.

The first securing of the forehead side around the head *over* the back piece prevents the back roll from coming too high up, and if the fastening of this piece is done securely the whole ' cap ' feels very secure and comfortable.

The ' balance for the elaborate head-dress ' (page 103, No. 7) is a practical comment upon an historic impossibility ! The angle at which these tall toppling steeples remain poised challenges all the laws of gravity ; when from the extreme tip depends a large gauze veil the leverage must have been terrific and the drag upon the small hairs over the forehead is known. We know that the ladies wore certain close-fitting caps *under* these steeples—first a linen cap, then a black velvet affair, then a gauze cap with a stiffened edge shading the face and special loops and marks over the forehead that announced the wearer's social status and bank balance, etc. We cannot guarantee that the construction shown was the exact mediæval method of procedure, but something of the kind was inevitable and this proves reasonably com-

fortable.   Bind the hair on to the extreme top of the head into a tight
' bun,' placing this knob rather to the *front* above the eyebrows.   Place
a ' soup-plate ' circle of fine gauze with a stiffened edge over the whole
head, placing it well forward so that the ' rim ' touches the neck at the
back and projects forward over the face in front (secure it to the hair
and knob).   Then take a strip of black velvet and pull it tightly over
the hair knob in front and tie it tightly behind the head—this strip
should be double and wide enough to come about three inches forward
over the face.

See that this band is really secure : well fastened down to the hair
' knob ' above the forehead, and tightly knotted at the nape of the neck.
(The ends may sometimes hang down in front of the shoulders as
shown.)   Note that beneath the steeple the neck and bosom were often
more or less screened by a gorget of dark stuff (as —very slightly—on
page 102 (B)).

Now see that the ' steeple ' is a good tight fit and the lower rim is
lined with velvet *with the grain set upwards against the grain of the
velvet band*—it will give a good grip.

Pull the steeple on and wedge the tight top knot of hair well inside
the rim ; on top to the front.   Then pull the front piece of the velvet
band C forward, and—turning it backwards—secure it to the lower
front of the steeple at D.

If this point D comes (as it should) directly over the top point of
the hair brim the fastening through the steeple will penetrate right
through to the bun of hair and mechanically speaking the suspended
weight *is* supported at the point of greatest strain.   Note that these
steeple head-dresses might be coloured, but that the face edging was
nearly *always* white and the velvet *always* black.   Also check the
historic side carefully, as slight differences in make or manner of
wearing had great significance.

WORKING DETAILS (page 101).—Study the variety in the MS. pictures and see to it that in a crowd of mediæval working women the costumes are sufficiently varied. Also see to it that the women's occupations and properties are suitable and likely.

The distaff and spindle so permeate the mediæval picture that quite as important occupations are overlooked. One MS. describes the workmen's wives going out ' in a flock ' with their husbands' dinners wrapped up in clean white board cloths—cheese and chickens and bread, a pleasant picture. Be sure that your working women wear practical ' working ' clothes while attending to their tasks, with the resultant folds and wrinkles and marks of ' wear ' ; or else you will get mere ' fancy dress.'

The ' wear ' of the working clothes is part of the making ; the tucked-up skirts of the fisher-girl and the barefoot Irish Biddy with her full loose skirt and head-shawl are practically mediæval survivals.

Common sense should rule throughout. The tucked-up gown on the right (page 113, No. 3) is a variation from the usual method that suggests the figure was engaged in filling a creel or *back* basket that she would presently sling behind her back, when the skirt could be dropped again as she walked home. Otherwise, for work done between the feet, it would be obviously easier to have the fullness of the skirt tucked *behind* the figure. Also any action that raises the arms above the shoulder level necessitates the bodice being pulled up and ' bloused ' loosely over the belt. Shoes from the wet fields would be mud-caked (or in frost would probably show wisps of straw packing). Such mud-caked shoes would be taken off at the door of a ' good ' room or when sitting before the fire, and the automatic action of drawing off the damp, footless stockings and hanging them up to dry beside the fire would make bare feet indoors much more usual with the poor than the MS. pictures of them (out-of-doors) suggest.

The simple head-wrap can be variously adjusted and would hold the hair out of the eyes of a busy woman (No. 1, page 113). Put one short end, BC, around the head, knotting it on one side (BC) ; take the far end, AA, and wrap it around the neck, under the chin, and tuck the last end, A, up under the tight edge of the wrap over the opposite ear. The knot, BC, over the right ear should be covered by the first sweep of the cloth and the length of the whole wrap should allow of its passing once closely around the neck before tucking in the end, A.

The second turban effect (page 113, No. 2) is made from the same length of cloth. The side, BC, is placed around the forehead and the ends, BC, are tied behind the head. The back-piece, AA, is then lifted up and folded down over the forehead (AA), *enclosing* the knot, BC, and the corners, AA, are pushed in under the bulge of this knot at the nape of the neck. The figure (D) on page 105 shows this turban in wear—properly put on it gives a smooth cap effect. Cf. also p. 102 (D). Any hair should be knotted towards the back of the head and the first knot, BC, *may* be tied twice, enclosing this lump of hair and adding to the effect of size when the head is covered by the outer flap, AA.

'A shoe' needs no explanation and is easily copied. The white linen hood pattern is quickly made and easily slipped on and off. It is a tube, the lower open end of which covers the shoulders, and the top open end frames the face. This last will be found far too large, so that a slanting seam is shown which should be fitted *on* the wearer and run from the centre of the forehead over the top of the head and continues down the single seam of the tube.

The leather work-bag, box and basket for wool are all actual patterns from MS. and may be copied easily. The bag-neck is rucksack shaped with a covering flap—an *excellent* bag where a slow fumbling undoing is required—two fastenings to the flap and two ties within will occupy a long speech. The work-box is made from *one* piece of leather cut as the tar box on page 93, No. 14. The basket (when used) was full of brightly-coloured wools.

A metal ewer, wooden bath-tub (see this is bound by brown willow withes (*not* metal bands), a wooden soap-bowl (very modern) and towels are accurate properties.

The distaff and spindle may be made by any carpenter; also a mediæval wool winder and carding hands are shown—and modern 'hand' weavers would probably be able to supply them.

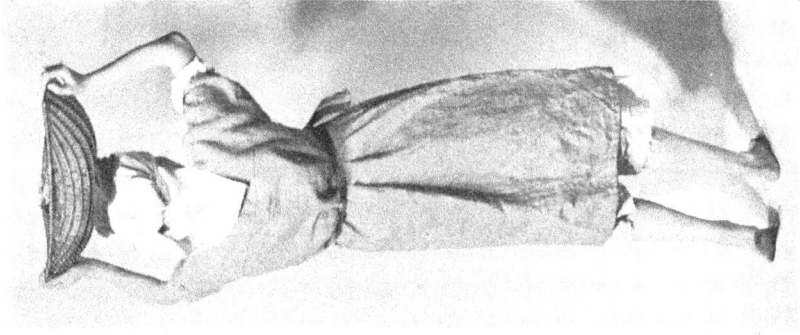

(C)

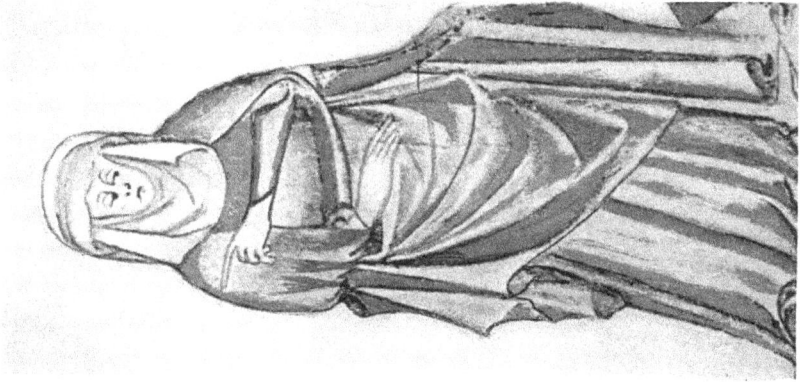

(B)

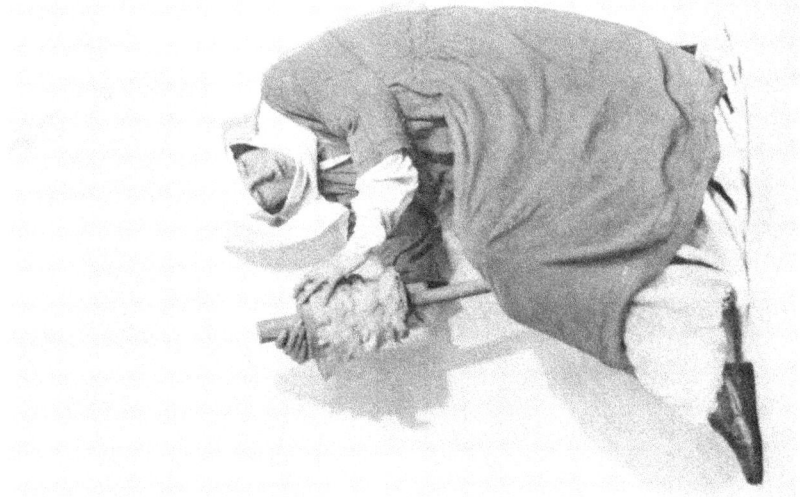

(A)

DRESSES OF MEDIÆVAL WORKING WOMEN   [B.M. MS. Egerton, 1894, 14c.]

Two (A), (C) made up ; (B) the original picture

(A)

(B)

(C)

(D)

(E)

(F)

WOMEN AT WORK AT VARIOUS OCCUPATIONS, FOURTEENTH AND FIFTEENTH CENTURIES

(A) (Note kerchief) [B.M. MS. Stowe 17, 14c.] (B) [B.M. MS. Harl. 6563, 14c.]

(C) [B.M. MS. Luttrell Psalter, 14c.] (D) [B.M. Facs. 162, 15c.]

(E) [Bodl. Liby. Ox. MS. Douce 6, 14c.] (F) [B.M. MS. Addl. 20698, 15c.]

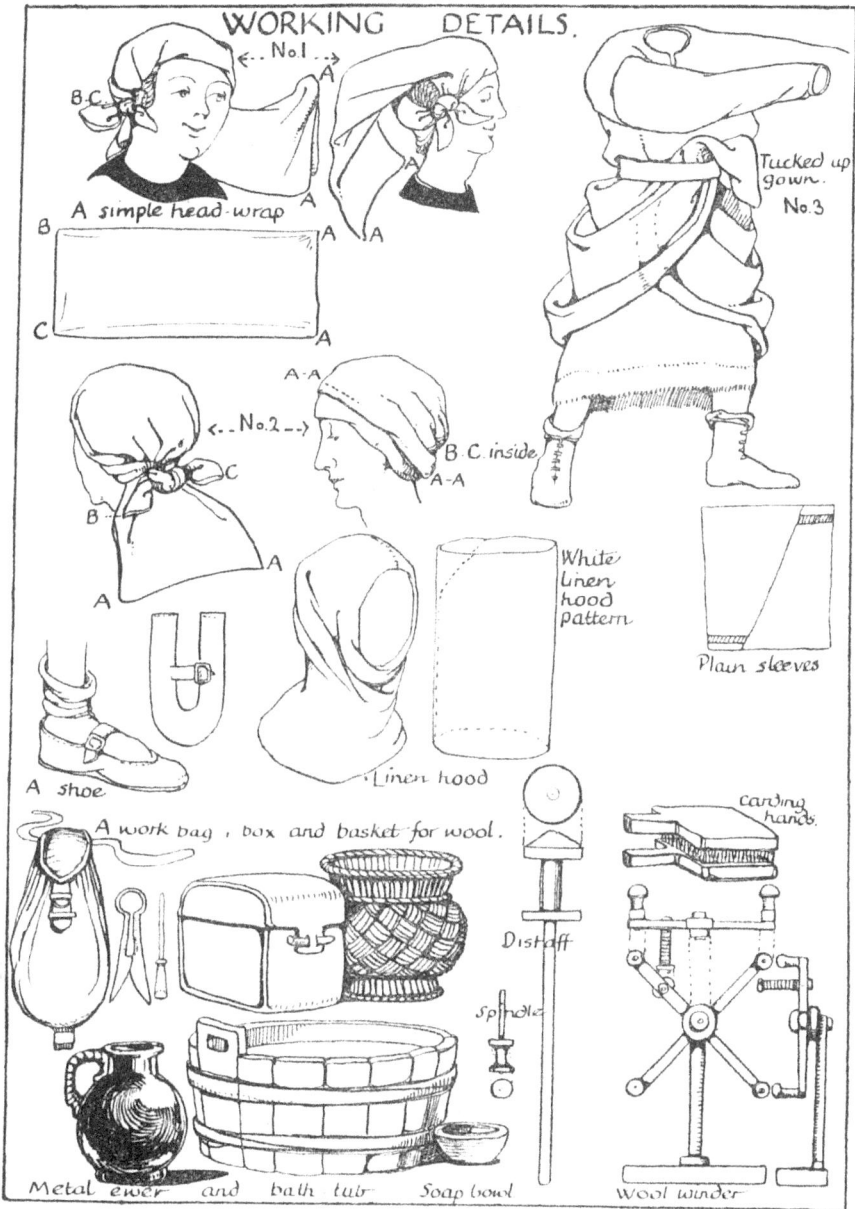

WORKING DETAILS.

No 1

B C

A

A simple head-wrap

B

A

C

A

Tucked up gown. No 3

No 2

C

B

A-A

B C inside

A-A

A

White linen hood pattern

Plain sleeves

A shoe

Linen hood

A work bag, box and basket for wool.

carding hands.

Distaff

Spindle

Metal ewer and bath tub   Soap bowl

Wool winder

DRESSES.—A word may well be said concerning the mediæval
ladies' underwear ; though it was not so much in evidence as it is—
especially for stage purposes—to-day.   The wear of the clothes has
been emphasised throughout, and it is utterly impossible to get the
correct carriage for an old dress when wearing modern ' undies '.   The
mediæval ideal (exaggerated in the late fourteenth and fifteenth
centuries) was a straight back and forward carriage of the body such
as is obtained by walking with the weight on the heels of a flat slipper.
Always where you get very ornate clothing, the remarkable head-
dresses, long pointed toes to the shoes, etc., you get an equally elaborate
posture.   (We do not say that the curiously upheld hands of the
mediæval ladies were a constant gesture, but do point out that they
indicate a movement entirely appropriate to the costume.)   In the
early periods the lady wears a long chemise-like smock and stockings
gartered below the knee, so low that the rolled-over tops would show
if she lifted her skirt high in running (page 115 f.).   When lacing first
begins, it is no more than a drawing together of the robe at the back or
sides into a closer fit.   Under these loose dresses there should be no
attempt at corsetry, nor any treatment of the material which gives a
smooth effect : the wrinkles across the body and small folds which
form in wear are a definite part of the costume.[1]   The later, more
elaborate robes, such as those worn on pages 101 and 102, were obviously worn over some sort of corset, doubtless in the nature of a broad,
belt-like band round the middle of the body to which bodice and skirt
may be securely attached, thus preventing the belt and bodice fitments
from slipping out of place.   Do not attempt to pull this corset down
over the hips ; it is as far removed from the long-waisted Elizabethan
corset (which kept the wearer unbendable between bust and thigh) as
the Elizabethan corset is from the Victorian one, which permits of a
bend at the waist.   Without troubling the costume designer with too
many unnecessary details, we would merely point out that it is impossible to get the correct effect by copying the outside of any dress
without understanding the underlying structure.

[1] Yet something like *smocking* appears to have been known in the twelfth
century.

(A)

(B)

(C)

(E)

(D)

(F)

(G)

A Miscellaneous Page of Varying Attitudes in Dress or Undress, with Accessories
(A) [B.M. Facs. 233, 15c.]   (B) [V. & A. M. Facs. Psautier, Bibl. Nat. Paris, 14c.]
(C) [B.M. MS. Addl. 38120, 15c.]   (D) [B.M. MS. Luttrell Psalter, 14c.]
(E) [Bodl. Liby. Ox. MS. Miracles of Virgin]   (F) [B.M. Facs. 72. II. about 10c.]
(G) [B.M. Cott. MS. Nero C. IV. 12c.]

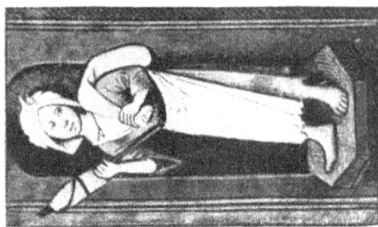

(C)

(F)

(B)

(E)

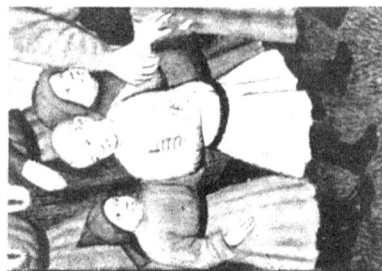

(A)

(D)

BABIES AND CHILDREN OF THE FOURTEENTH AND FIFTEENTH CENTURIES

(A) [B.M. Facs. 183-6, 15c.] (B) [Bodl. Liby. MS. Douce 6, 14c.] (C) [B.M. MS. Harl. 4425, 15c.]

(D) [B.M. Roy. MS. 2. B. VII. 14c.] (E) [V. & A. M. Facs. 15c.] (F) [Bodl. Liby. MS. Douce 311, 15c.]

CHILDREN

THE mediæval child was frequently born on a straw bed on the floor, whereupon the mother removed (circumstances permitting) to her own bed and was presently refreshed with the daintiest food available ; the babe meanwhile being tubbed in warm water and towelled by the fire ; a ceremony of constant recurrence in contemporary art.

Infants in arms were early wrapped in swaddling clothes, their tender pates protected by close coifs or linen wraps ; and for greater safety they were for the greater part of the time strapped to carrying-boards (as on page 119, No. 2). All these impedimenta were rarely removed save for necessary ablutions and changes.

The crib shown on page 119, No. 1, is light, convenient and comfortable, and easy to make : two handle holes cut in the semi-circular wooden ends make it easy to lift and carry about—*or* to 'hang upon the tree top.' The ends are 'rockers,' and two straps over the top hold the occupant in. To make the bed, lay some covering over the long open sticks, put down a little bag of chopped straw, pad with loose clean wool ; then wrap up your baby in a linen sheet and tuck him up comfortable under a woolly blanket. There may be a small feather pillow (it must be stuffed with hen feathers or down—*never* with the spiky boned feathers of flight birds !).

In various MS. cradles of this sort are shown carried under the arm like a basket or balanced on the head of the working woman ; one woman is shown standing with upraised arm, but the action looks more reassuring than necessary. A poorer baby has no cradle, but is tied to a board padded with wool ; and another seems to be carried in a wicker basket.

The Madonna, alone in mediæval art, seems the only mother allowed to nurse her child comfortably and naturally.

Children from the time they were fairly able to walk and talk or, say, from about the age of two, wore a simplified edition of the clothing of their parents, with this difference : that little boys, till they were 'breeched,' dressed to all intents and purposes like little girls. Between four and six both sexes became practically miniature editions of their elders. Rarely (before the sixteenth century) were the worst freaks of fashion inflicted on them till they reached the age of about twelve. Even in very 'smart' circles, girls commonly wore their own long hair flowing loose, sometimes up to about fifteen or sixteen, throughout the greater part of the Middle Ages.

The two children shown at play on page 119, No. 3 (redrawn from a twelfth-century MS.) evidently belong to the well-to-do class. Yet (possibly as a concession to youth) the younger has bare feet and the elder boy apparently bare legs in shoes of undressed leather. The gathering around the sleeves we believe to be smocking—it looks like smocking in the drawing, and comes at a point where smocking would be convenient in the dress. The pattern is therefore very simple to follow: two straight pieces, back and front, are gathered into two straight shoulder bands, cut slightly wider than the shoulders so as to bring the top smocking of the sleeve around the narrowest part of the upper arm.

Arrange the gathers into the bands, giving plenty of fullness either side, but keeping the end, at the sleeve-tops and just below the chin, fairly flat.

Sew the bands together along the width of the shoulders (page 119, No. 5), leaving an ample neck opening (page 119, No. 5). The sleeves are the two halves of a square, the width of the material (page 119, No. 5); they may conveniently be shaped slightly and are then gathered into bands at top and wrist and set into the dress *over* the ends of the neck bands (page 119, No. 5). A tooled leather belt with single slot fastening finishes the dress.

The elder boy's is similar, but the body part is cut in one without gathers and the neck fastened over in front by a single button. Do not cut a slit for this opening but turn the small triangular fold (that forms naturally in front of a loose neck opening) to the side and button down on to the side of the neck edge. Make the buttonhole through both thicknesses of cloth and sew the botton on to the edge of the neck.

This dress, of thinner material, is cut from pattern, page 119, No. 6 ; it is worn over a white linen slip. The shorter dress is usually worn over leggings, but all ' leggings ' seem to be wriggled off for games indoors (having tried all sorts of leggings, ancient and modern, we are convinced of this).

The simple head-dress shown on page 119, No. 4, is made of a single piece of linen knotted once. Place the *middle* of the stuff on the crown of the head with one end (BB) hanging down in front and the other (AA) behind, fold back BB over head till the doubled fold of linen comes just above the eyebrows, and then bring the corners, BB, round the head and knot in front as shown ; thus giving two thicknesses on top, a thick frill over the eyes and a flap, AA, over the hair behind.

A number of curiously ' modern ' mediæval toys are also shown on page 119.

CHILDREN.

The baby's cradle
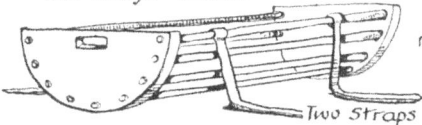

The baby in it
No 1
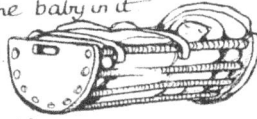

Two straps to hold baby in

Poor baby strapped to board No·2

A simple wimple for a little girl Make it in white linen

No 4
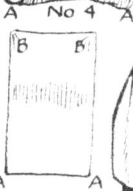

No·3

re drawn from an old manuscript

Neck yoke
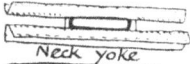

No·6

Sleeve
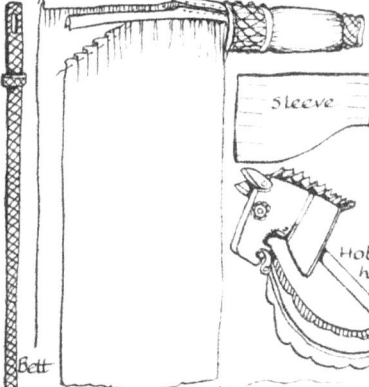

Hobby horse

Belt

No·5

Spin top

Coloured pin wheel

wooden soldier

Leather Doll
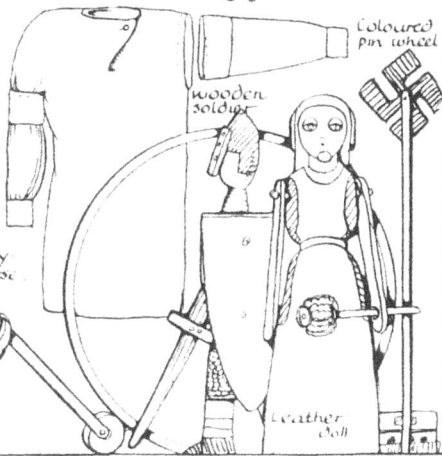

'GOD SAVE YOU, PILGRIM, WHITHER ARE YOU BOUND?'
Fully equipped for the start

TRAVELLERS AND PILGRIMS

As already mentioned, the one pattern often serves for rich and poor alike, according to the material and trimmings used. Thus MSS. etc. show us garments of the type of cloak, No. 3, page 123, used—in heavy rich brocade and fur—as Court dress. Omit the hood and carry out a black and white scheme, with under-robe black, lining and belt white, etc.; and a very striking effect will be gained that could equally well be used for a statesman's gown. (We repeat again, for travellers as for others, we give the plain pattern, best fitted for the character, so that it may be adapted and used in copying the—apparently—more elaborate robes shown in the MS. Dressmakers and others will readily understand this.)

The Traveller, page 123, No. 1, wears the ordinary mediæval robe explained on page 21, Nos. 1, 2 and 3. No. 2 might be used as an alternative (cf. p. 57, No. 1).

The Cloak, No. 3 (page 123), is made from a double of cloth, the fold coming at the neck; this double is so shaped (on the figure) that it appears as a seam beginning at the neck, following the slope of the shoulder well over the deltoid and running into the side seam. The front 'slits' should be marked on the figure *before* cutting—care being taken not to carry them too high (a little *below* the level of the shoulder curve on stout figures)—and the front width should be kept as narrow as possible.

As shown, the belt fastens *over* the front piece, leaving the back piece free to swing as a cloak. A hood may be made after patterns on pages 57 and 93 and the felt hat (page 123, No. 1) has strings to tie it on, knotted around the crown, or when in use passed through little holes above the ears and tied under the chin.

The scrip is made like a modern child's school satchel, of leather, fastening with wooden buttons.

Sandals are worn. The pilgrim's staff, No. 4, page 123, should be studied carefully and historically. Various shrines gave various tokens (only Compostella had shells; don't use them promiscuously) and various routes produced their own water-bottles, so be sure your pilgrim goes the right road, if you know it.

No. 5, page 123, shows how to load and ride a donkey—the long bolster-shaped bag is filled equally at both ends through a slit in the centre that comes (in use) across the donkey's back. If these ' ends ' are packed full, they rise level with the donkey's back and form a flat platform upon which the washing basket can rest. The rider sits sideways behind the load.

The Horse rider frequently leads a second horse carrying the baggage, but when only one horse is used the load goes behind the saddle. The saddle shape (page 123, No. 13) shows how well adapted it was for such packing.

There was always a thick padding blanket over the horse under the saddle. This hangs down just beyond the horse's belly, under the rider's legs ; over this would be a smaller leather square, over this the padded wooden saddle (variously made for various purposes), over this the saddle cushion, with pockets. The ' foot mantle ' was seemingly no more than a blanket placed over the whole saddle before mounting and then wrapped round the waist, enfolding the feet and legs very comfortably. The stirrups were conveniently large. The bridle and bit varied and so should be closely noted when copying any definite period or type of horse. For the same reason the curious spiked horseshoes seen in many MS. should *not* be used indiscriminately. They were chiefly used for war horses, trained to fight by rearing and striking out with their front feet ; *not* for peaceful amblers. The Wheelbarrow, page 123, No. 7, is shown on page 83, No. 6.

The Shoes are all copies from MS. of travellers. Page 123, No. 12, shows a useful general pattern easily copied in various materials for different purposes.

Take a triangle of leather (lined or otherwise) A-B-B, place the foot as shown : with the heel in the centre of the side B-B and the toes pointing to the apex A. Close up the back seam B and beginning at the toe A, close up the front over the toes and instep—shaping to the fullness of the foot (exactly as a cook pinches up the paste over a Cornish pasty) ; the top edge may be turned down to show the coloured lining, and a little shaping of the heel seam will give a neat ankle. For elaborate shoes the front may be gold-laced or decorated as desired. The wooden clog, page 123, No. 9, is cut from a single block of wood (alder is waterproof) and the broad leather band nailed into a loop, shaped to the foot. Originally worn by herdsmen in marshy fields, in the fourteenth century they were adopted by ' the quality ' for walking in wet weather. Van Eyck's portrait of Arnolfini in the National Gallery shows a pair of typical clogs with a photographic detail that repays study.

TRAVELLERS AND PILGRIMS.

No 1

ROBE No·2

Tokens
Food
No·4

Pilgrims
Staff

and
drink

Cloak
No 3

No 5

No 6

Foot
mantle

No·7

No 14

Traveller wearing cloak No 3

Sitting on a donkey
load in front

Riding on a horse
packages behind

A side laced shoe
No·8

Wooden clog
No·9

Stout walking
boot. No 10

B B

Saddle
No·13

A

Pattern for an easy walking shoe
No·12

No·11

Riding boot with spur

(A) (B)

(C) (D)

(E) (F)

LATE MEDIÆVAL HORSE TRAVELLERS AND A WAGGON WITH ROLLED COVERING
(A) [B.M. MS. Addl. 12228, 13c.]   (B) [B.M. Roy. MS. 2. B. VII. 14c.]
(C) [B.M. Roy. MS. 18. D. II. 15c.]   (D) [B.M. Facs. 77, 15c.]
(E) [B.M. Facs. 100, 15c.]   (F) [B.M. Roy. MS. 17. A. II. 15c.]

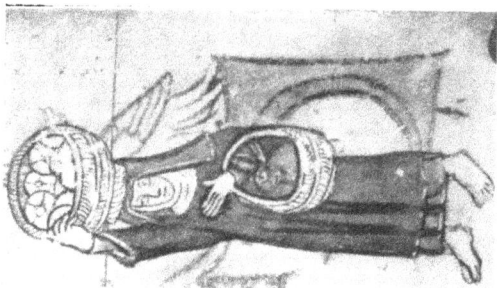

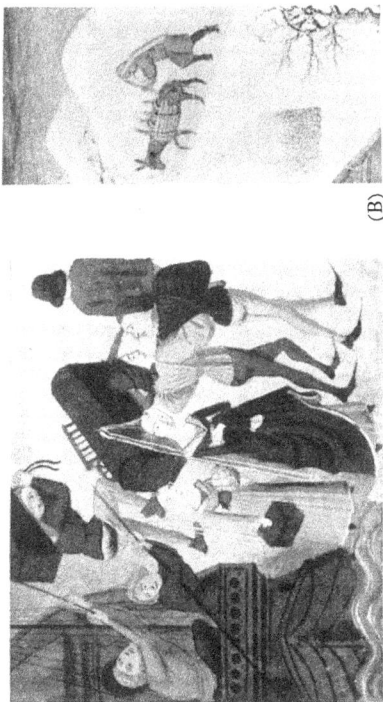

STUDIES IN DISEMBARKING AND COUNTRY FOLK GOING TO MARKET

(A) [B.M. MS. Harl. 4380, 15c.]   (B) [B.M. Facs. 59, 15c.]   (C) [B.M. MS. Stowe 17, 14c.]

(D) [B.M. Facs. 77, 15c.]   (E) [B.M. MS. Addl. 35315, 15c.]

(A)

(B)

FIFTEENTH-CENTURY HORSE LITTER AND BAGGAGE TRANSPORT

(A) [B.M. Facs. 77, 15c.]   (B) [Facs. V. & A. M. 93. D. 52 (*Chroniques de Charlemagne*, J. van der Gheyn), 15c.]

BOOTS AND SHOES

NOTE that conspicuously ' piked ' shoes and ' boots ' were not typical of the Middle Ages *at large*. They were never more than a freak of fashion, noticeable *c.* 1380-1400 and again *c.* 1460. There is *written* evidence also of exaggerated points about the last years of the eleventh and the first third or so of the twelfth, but illustrations are rare. For the rest, mediæval footwear, though in the better classes generally more or less pointed, only emphasizes the natural contour of the foot, the point being a mere accentuation of the line of the big toe. More rounded toes, however, are found at most periods, though usually conforming to the outline of the foot. Heels in the modern sense were unknown, though a slight scooping out of the sole would appear to have been needed below the instep for the firmer fixing of the under-leather of the spur. *N.B.*—The spurs with exaggerated shanks only had their *raison d'être*, strictly speaking, with the cap-à-pié plate armour worn in the field or the lists. During the greater part of the Middle Ages, the tall boots (specimens appear from the thirteenth century) had the leg and ' vampy ' cut in a single piece of leather. From the close of the fourteenth century these were increasingly cut separately. The better classes wore the boot shaped to the leg, laced or clasped up the side ; or, alternatively, the extra fullness at the small of the leg was caught back in a broad fold and buckled down.[1]

Note.—Ordinary travellers' gear should not be confounded with that peculiar to pilgrims pure and simple.

The former was normally as comfortable and convenient as means would permit. Some pilgrims travelled at ease, combining pleasure with piety. Others undertook the journey in a severely penitential spirit, reflected in their outer man.

---

[1] Clearly explained, with patterns, in Harmand : *Jeanne d'Arc*, pp. 179-182.

INVALIDS

A WRAPPER and cap are worn by invalids and their pillows and bedding appear very modern and comfortable. The drawings on page 131 explain details that may be of use.

The leper's equipment was a long gown covering him completely, with a hood attached, and he had large over-shoes and gloves which he might not remove when with any clean men. He must not touch handrails over bridges or stairways or anything that was used by others without first putting on his gloves. He must carry his own mug and bowl and when buying wine or receiving drink it must be poured directly into his mug—he must not touch the bottle or jack. He must drink from streams below the level of other houses and must hand nothing to any child or grown-up person. In giving money it must be thrown to him and in making payment he must place his coin in a bowl of vinegar and water.

The wooden clapper was more usual than a bell. He must sound it continuously and pass all people on the windward side.

(A) (B)

(C)

A CRIPPLE, AND BEDSIDE MINISTRATIONS
(A) [Bodl. Liby. Ox. MS. 264, 14c.]   (B) [B.M. MS. Harl. 4425, 15c.]
(C) [B.M. Facs. 197, 15c.]

(D)

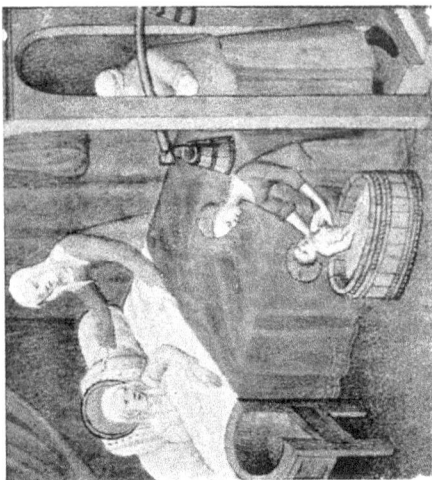

(B)

(C)

(A)

MORE BEDSIDE CARE AND STUDIES OF THE AFFLICTED

(A) [B.M. Roy. MS. 15, D. I. 15c.]   (B) [B.M. MS. Harl. 2897, 15c.]   (C) [B.M. Roy. MS. 13. B. VIII. 12c.]   (D) B.M. Facs. 1837, 15c.]

Wooden clapper

Wooden mug

over-boot

For a leper.

Leather gloves

Wooden clapper

Hut enclosure and sign.

Mirror and Comb.

A bed in an alcove

Pillow cases

Stone slab movable fire place and skillet

Cooking pot

Straw pallet

Raised cradle

Horn and badge for beggars

Splints and bandages

Leg-rest

A crutch

Crawling block.

A bath with tent hung from ceiling

Begging bowl

and bandaged legs

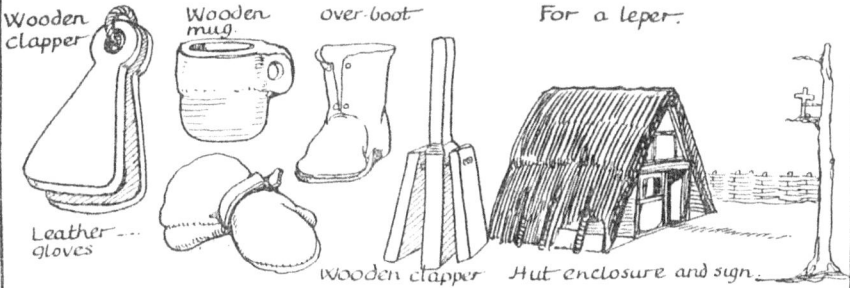

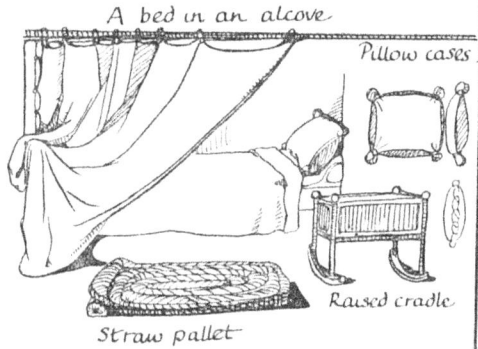

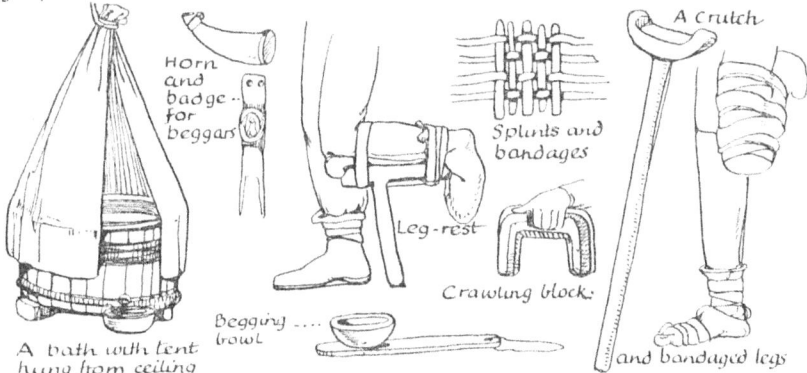

BEGGARS, CRIPPLES &
TOILET ACCESSORIES

PEACE AND WAR

THIS section is largely devoted to material taken from Anglo-Saxon sources, as the pre-Conquest period has hitherto been somewhat neglected and the student is apt to be at a loss for guidance.

First consider the settings and when dealing with a definite locality study the landscape carefully, believing the historic references implicitly, as woods and swamps vanish and ponds and mill-cuts fill up. Specially note the smaller water-courses, dykes, fords, etc., that so often come into the ' story,' as these sometimes cause troublesome puzzles by changing position.

On the whole Forest was smaller and more twisted and clearings and building showed *axe* work. This is important, as it gives the design note of sharp triangular cuts, and *almost* eliminates planks. Fencing is wattle and, when daubed and plastered, was used for building. Note sheds thatched with local reed, heather or straw, and circular pens of wattle, or dry stone diking; fencing of *split* paling and withes. Benches by the door may be split logs, semicircular side down, and four legs strutted at a good angle. The garden may be a little distance from the hut, and well fenced, with a lych-gate entrance. Herding and field work are shown; dogs were small; sheep mostly hairy and horned, horses small and cobby (except war-horses). See to it the colour of the people's clothing approximates to the landscape and weather (chalk, red earth, sand, etc.) especially about the boots (see general note).

INTERIORS.—The huts are small with earthen floors; often a wood and wickerwork staircase *or slope* (like a hen plank) leads to the upper loft. Fireplaces large, a flat stone in the centre under a smoke hole (or against a wall, where we believe a wooden cowl was used). Sleeping benches or shut-in beds are against the walls; stools and benches are *well made* though heavy. An iron cauldron and a few pottery cooking-jars stand by the fireplace and some rakes and wooden farm implements may be hung on the walls, also a skin pegged to a board,

(A)

(B)

(C)

PROCESSION AND GATHERINGS OF NOBLES AND ROYALTY OF THE LATE FIFTEENTH
CENTURY

(A)   [B.M. Facs. 77, 15c.]   (B)   [B.M. MS. 15c.]

(C)   [B.M. Roy. MS. 15. E. IV. 15c.]

The Scene and Crowd at a City Execution in the Fifteenth Century

some bundles of herbs, and bacon and hams hung up near the smoke hole. There must be a chest for storing bread, cloths, etc. ; this may form a seat by the fire. Colour may be used in flat painting in any of the three primary colours—yellow, red, blue, with white and black, but *very* simply. There are practically no hangings, though hides and leather may be used to cover entrances or benches, or spread on the floor if there are children. Keep the hut effect as low as possible and get the smoke-hung atmosphere above, to give the firelighting at dusk. The Hall is the only large building ; the fire is low, being sunk below the level of the ground in the central furrow, and the whole floor space is usually below ground level, the entrance steps leading down into the hall.

Behind were the sleeping bunks and it will be seen how readily the space between any two pillars could be screened off to provide a small side-chamber, suitable for an invalid, a clerk, a special meeting place.

The shadows of the pillars falling back into the raised partitions and up the walls are very effective, giving a spreading processional effect when a light is carried between them.

The daïs table is at the end, it may be slightly raised, and hung around with draught-curtains, giving side shadows ; incidentally, do a little research here, according to your especial needs, as in some cases the doctor, harpist, or magician shares this upper part of the hall with the owner.

The lower tables are placed on either side by the columns : trestle-boards and benches easily moved. Cords raise a lighted lamp to the roof-tree above the daïs table, circular shields and arms hang upon pillars and walls ; beware of grouping metal spears, etc., near the fire. Remember in furniture-making the *axe*-shaping of the pieces ; and see that the axes are long-handled with sharply curved heads. This insisting upon the old method of production gives an understanding of the materials with which you design for the period.

Woodwork and plaster may be painted and gold used sparingly, chiefly on the daïs table and surroundings. White linen and coloured cloths and skins may be used, elaborate bowls of bronze and copper and enamel, and some glass. The whole effect is utilitarian and com-fortable ; there is nothing rough or coarse. Aim for a squarely de-signed simplicity ; a large sense of strong pillars, squarely built tables and benches, circular shields and straight spears and hangings ; then add sparingly, in a few well chosen places, as much rich barbaric splendour as you consider fit.

Thus also in costume : the wife, bringing in her husband from the fields to dress and greet guests, urges him into clean plain white linen, plain dark coat and hose; dark woollen cloak, etc.; and all sombre and plain except, as the saga mentions, the scarlet shoes and straps, and the lines give a sense of polished buckles and shining golden hair.

The cloak is fastened with a circular brooch or ring-knot of gold. Circular gold neck ornaments were worn, and the Saxon kings seem often to have worn a circlet of gold.

The under-dress was of linen, long-sleeved to the wrist, and covered by a second of darker linen or wool; the whole held in at the hips or worn with a belt. The cloak may be short or long and fastened usually upon the shoulder.

The legs below the knee were often clad in hose, or wrapped over with cloth and bound up with thongs. Most labourers went bare-legged, but usually socks and shoes were worn, the custom varying according to the district.

Though the upper lip was shaved, beards were worn long, as also the hair, carefully parted and frequently curled into shining ringlets. Bare heads were the rule, though caps were sometimes worn for travel, or perhaps in a wind or out hunting, to keep the hair from the eyes.

Illustrations of defensive body-armour are rare before the Norman period. Most warriors, as depicted, content themselves with helmet and shield. The former was mostly conical or of ' Phrygian ' shape, formed of a metal framework, lined with horn, leather or segments of metal; the latter of leather over wood, rimmed and reinforced with metal, with a large central metal boss. There is, however, evidence sufficient that the best-armed wore short-sleeved byrnies of mail, or metal, horn or leather scales.

It is well to look carefully into the colour notes of the Saxon period, as it changed in significance. Canute and the Danish kings mark a preponderance of black. After 1066 the Norman colours came into the Saxon scheme. You will have to work the colours, largely from references in the text, as the MSS. have but few coloured drawings, and the ornamental colours used have little or no reference to the material.

The later description of a wooden plough by Gervase Markham shows the main portions unchanged. In the early example shown (A) (page 140), the main plough beam is raised to an improbable height. In principle there was the main solid plough beam chosen from a log of wood so bent that when the heavy end lay upon the ground the lighter end was raised at a height convenient to the ploughman's hand. This end was thinned down and grasped by the two hands, and seems to suggest a short thick crossbar at this handle end. To this main beam was fixed (below) the ground cutter of the plough and at an angle above and in front of this the upright cutter. From above and between them, at a convenient angle, came the beam or draught traces to which the oxen were harnessed. The plough is an interesting study, but, as not likely to be used, we pass to the sower on the right. He wears one single shirt-garment and his hopper is slung around his neck by a broad band of linen or leather. There will be another band behind his back to steady the load against his chest, and if he is using both arms, the motion follows the rhythm of his footsteps, the alternate arm being outflung between each two steps. If the corn bag is of linen, bind it upon a withy rim to hold it open. The corn measure (upon the left) suggests that a wooden measuring 'strike' was in use in Saxon times. The scytheman has bare feet and a wide-brimmed straw hat (see page 140, (A)).

Note that in each of these three workers the shirt swings clear above the knees. It alters the whole character of this light active Saxon garment if the knee joint makes a break in its jaunty swing.

Page 140 (B).—As mannequin in a costume-book the wearer (B) seems rather left out in the cold, but his loom is a good working study. The cloth (so conveniently tilted to show the pattern) would actually lie horizontally before him.

Page 140 (C).—The shepherd sits upon the hillside with his horn. The MS. suggests that these are ox-horns of the very largest size.

Page 140 (D).—A plunge churn. The original plunge churn was probably shaped out of a single block of wood but the earliest examples show cooper work—the plunger which was thrust up and down through the milk (exactly as a cream mixer is used in the modern milk transport cans of to-day) had a wooden head and a splash top of wood or leather, the height of the churn. For a design of this, see page 140, (D). Incidentally, churning was *not* a sitting-down job, as the exasperated gesture of the waiting dairymaid shows.

Milk pails were usually small and deep with a handle up one side (like a Scots 'handy' to-day), but the figure on the right risks a wooden bowl raised upon a stool. (*N.B.*—the goat lifts its eye and grins.)

ILLUSTRATIONS (page 139).—(A) shows the large deeply-feathered arrows (piercing the leather and metal shields) and a double-headed battle-axe. (B) is an armourer honing up a long sword; the great length and size of these ponderous blades are well shown both in (B) and (C), where the sword is being ground (eleventh century).

(E) (mid-thirteenth century) gives excellent detail for the forge. Practically the same make of anvil, tongs and hammer, etc., are in use to-day and there is characteristic action in the smith squinting down the blade when truing it up. Note the leather aprons. The worker upon the left has loosened the strings of his coif. He is fashioning a typical helm of the period, while behind him a third man is filing away the rough edges of the finished article. Note on extreme left the war-horse's field-armour : a trapper and headstall of linked mail.

(D) and (F) (of the third quarter of the fifteenth century) show siege-warfare. Note in (D) the scaling of the enemy's walls under cover of archery-fire. The archers and crossbowmen wear light half-armour with sallets or ' tin-hats,' the storming party carrying shields as a protection against missiles from above. The typical satchel for the crossbowman's bolts is well shown. In (F) the preliminary attack is engaged. Across the river a piece of field ordnance is being trained on the town walls. Note the armour and characteristic action of the crossbowmen. The device of a ' fire-steel ' on their bolt-quivers marks them for Burgundian troops.

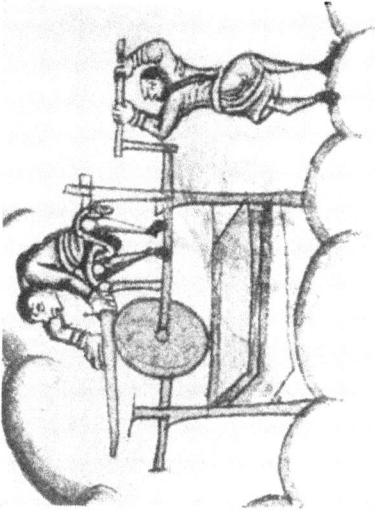

(C)

(B)

(A)

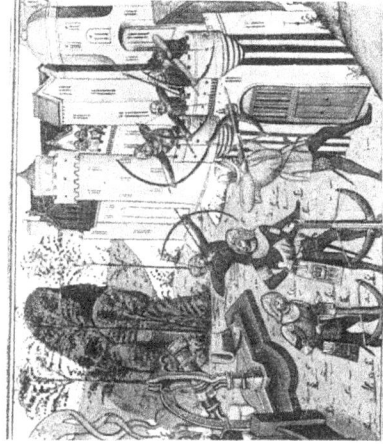

(F) [Trin. C. Camb. MS. O. 9. 34. 13c.]

(E) [B.M. Roy. MS. 14 E. IV. 15c.]

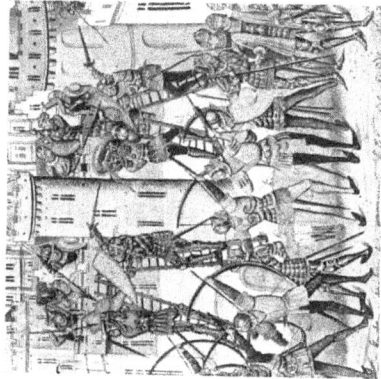

(D)

WEAPONS AND WARFARE FROM THE ELEVENTH TO THE FIFTEENTH CENTURIES

(D) & (F) [Trin. C. Camb. MS. R. 17. 1. 11c.]

(A), (B), (C) [Trin. C. Camb. MS. R. 17. 1. 11c.]

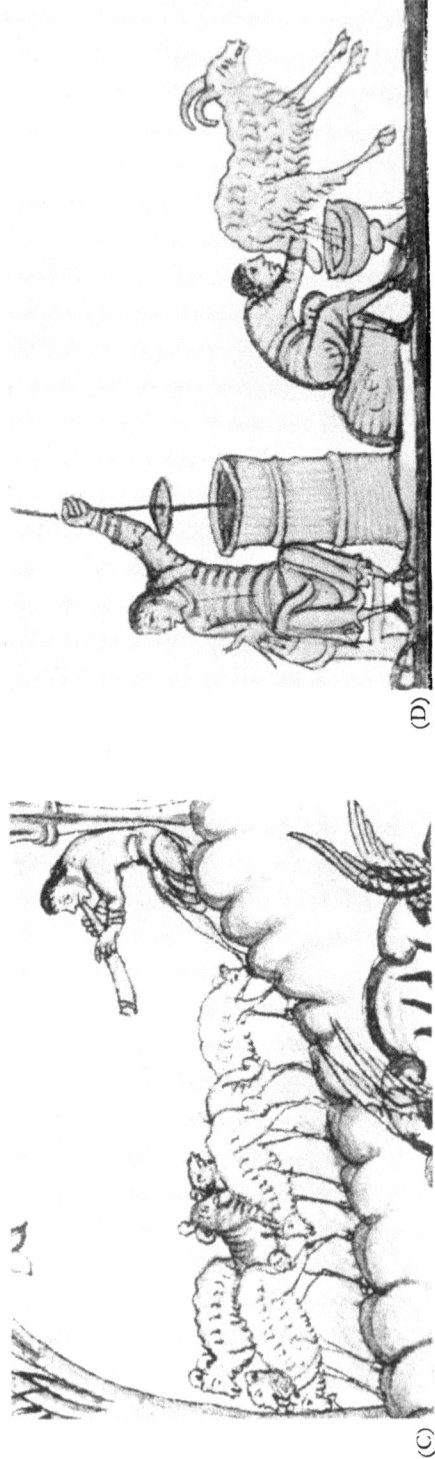

(A), (C), (D) [Trin. C. Camb. MS. R. 17. 1. 11c.]   (B) [Trin. C. Camb. MS. O. 9. 34. 13c.]

SAXON FIELD WORKERS, AND A THIRTEENTH CENTURY LOOM

INDEX TO TEXT AND ILLUSTRATIONS

NOTE.—*All references to illustrations are printed in heavy type. 'ph.' denotes a photograph of a living model or piece of sculpture; 'patt.' is a line drawing of a pattern; the rest of the references in heavy type is to reproductions from MSS., but accessories are almost all indexed from plates of drawings.*

www.ingramcontent.com/pod-product-compliance
Lightning Source LLC
Chambersburg PA
CBHW032001040426
42448CB00006B/443